WITNESS TO THE DARK
A Testimony of Survival

Wolf Holles

gefen
publishing house בית הוצאה לאור
JERUSALEM ● NEW YORK   Est. 1981

Cover Design: Leah Ben Avraham/ Noonim Graphics
Typesetting: www.optumetech.com

ISBN: 978-965-7023-90-7

1 3 5 7 9 8 6 4 2

Gefen Publishing House Ltd.
6 Hatzvi Street
Jerusalem 9438614,
Israel
972-2-538-0247
orders@gefenpublishing.com

Gefen Books
c/o Baker & Taylor Publisher Services
30 Amberwood Parkway
Ashland, Ohio 44805
516-593-1234
orders@gefenpublishing.com

www.gefenpublishing.com

Printed in Israel
Library of Congress Control Number: 2022904090

Contents

Part Three – Are We Free Yet?

Part Four – The Lost Train

Part Five – Will We Ever Get Home?

Prologue

As the end of World War II approached, efforts were made at many Nazi concentration camps to destroy records and either to murder the remaining prisoners or to transfer them elsewhere. This was in response to SS instructions that no prisoners should be found when Allied troops arrived.

The "death marches" are infamous, but less well known is that there were also many transfers by train. These transports were frequently conducted from within the camps themselves. When the Allied armies smashed beyond the Rhine and began slicing into central Germany, in early April 1945, three trains left Bergen-Belsen. One reached its destination in Theresienstadt. The second was liberated by the Americans at a village near Farsleben in Germany. The last of the three transports, the one we were on, was the last train to leave Bergen-Belsen. It never reached its destination.

Our train contained about twenty-five hundred Jews – men, women, and children – and a group of armed SS guards. We were all loaded into forty-five railway cars. Some were passenger cars and some were typical antiquated freight cars called "forty and eights," signifying that these cars would accommodate forty men or eight horses. I was thirteen years old when I climbed with my mother and two brothers onto this train.

The armed SS guards, striding around the platform, kept motioning for the prisoners to move, yelling over the noise of truck engines, "*Vorwärts! Schneller!* Move it! Faster! Get it moving! Get it moving!"

The question on everyone's lips was "Where are we going?"

Nobody knew where. We had heard the name Theresienstadt. But where was it? A little dot on the world map. And who knew what was in store for us there?

In fact, our train never got to Theresienstadt in northwestern Czechoslovakia. Airstrikes by the Allies caused us to amble aimlessly through eastern Germany until we ended up at the destroyed Elstertal Bridge near the Czech border. Nobody – neither the British nor the Americans – knew where we were. That's why the train was known as the Lost Train.

PART ONE

In the Beginning

ONE

⁓

Before the War

Life in Germany was a paradise, Moeder (Mother) once told me. A paradise? Was she kidding? But I knew she was talking about Germany during the "golden years," between 1923 and 1929. In those days, the economy was robust and the country was experiencing something of a cultural renaissance, including an explosion of cinematic, cabaret, and theater activities in the so-called Weimar Republic. Life in Nürnberg, Moeder would often say wistfully, a melancholic look coming over her face, was great back then. Jewish people felt integrated and safe. They were proud of being German citizens. That was in the years before Hitler's rise to power, before he became the chancellor of Germany in 1933.

But then she would speak of the day she knew things had changed. She told this story often, as though in the telling she might alter the hurtful details. On a bitterly cold winter day, she was going across the street toward the bakery, where the owner – a middle-aged woman who routinely served my mother with a smile – now gave her a vicious look, snarling coldly, "*Jetzt sind ihr dran*" (Now it's your turn). And to my mother's horror, the owner added loudly, "Now we will get rid of all of you."

Not long after, Hitler was appointed chancellor. The SS started their chilling torchlight parades through the dark Nürnberg streets.

3

In 1933, my family left the country for Holland, which thankfully had opened its borders to Jewish refugees fleeing the rising tides of antisemitism in Germany.

My parents were both in their early thirties then, and we three boys were seven, five, and two years old. Life in the new country was not easy. There was widespread unemployment, and acclimation was tough – learning a new language, finding a new place to live, finding the right schools, adjusting to a new culture. But when my mother was recounting this part of our family history, Holland was already under German control, and the past was like a piece of precious jewelry that she kept in a secret box and took out from time to time to caress, to build our hope. I think of jewelry because in Holland my father dealt with wholesale jewelry, and Moeder helped him run the business. They had managed to put together for us a comfortable, middle-class lifestyle.

In the Netherlands, I remember, the winters were bitingly cold. In the morning, I'd fight my way out of the warm blankets. The room was always warm and cozy, and as I got dressed, I'd be captivated by the ice on the window panes frozen into shapes of flowers or trees. Another high point for us boys was gliding down the icy sidewalks.

Over the weekends, dressed warmly in winter jackets and woolen socks, our winter caps down over our ears, my friends and I would go ice skating. If I close my eyes, I can still feel my feet gliding over the ice, speeding across the frozen canals with the wind in my face (boy, was that great!).

In the warm summers, in the open fields hidden from the busy roads, I'd play soccer with school friends. It was the most popular sport in Holland, and I loved it. Wherever I went, in the streets or fields, on school grounds or in vacant lots, I could see neighborhood boys kicking balls across goal lines. I can recall sitting in the warm summer evening in the bleachers in Amsterdam watching excitedly as the soccer players competed in the Champions League. The soccer stars were our celebrities. We would collect cards featuring the big stars, and we traded them at school. We were immensely proud when we'd get a Kick Smit or Bert Caldenhove card – they were the magical ones.

When we were taken from our home, I longed for the freedom to run across a field, heading or kicking the ball. It's funny the things you miss when you're a prisoner.

There were other outdoor games that were great fun, games like volleyball or *bokje springen*, a leapfrog game. Yes, those were carefree childhood days, far away from the ugliness that in the near future would be happening all around me.

The day I had the awakening to how much danger we could have been in if we had not left Germany was when I walked into the living room and found my parents and brothers crouching before the radio listening tensely to Hitler's hysterical rapid-fire shrieking. This man, who was an Austrian, represented, my parents told me, the personification of evil. Only then did it dawn on me what this person was capable of doing. It was actually the first time that I heard the bone-chilling words of Hitler planning to annihilate the Jewish people in Europe. Just listening to this hateful diatribe, listening to him shouting in German, made chills run through me.

This was when we were on the brink of war. But months earlier, in 1938, in the wake of Kristallnacht, when a nationwide riot against Jews in Germany had been carried out and Hitler annexed the Sudetenland, the continent had begun preparing for war. A stream of Jewish refugees had already poured in from the German Reich, seeking refuge.

As the outbreak of war with Nazi Germany loomed larger, Dutch Jews began to line up at foreign consulates for visas and immigration papers. My father kept going to the US consulate in Amsterdam, hoping to get a visa. But the Great Depression had left countless millions unemployed, and the visa people at the consulate told my father that the annual immigration quota for the United States was practically filled. Jews (with minor exceptions) faced great difficulties getting into the United States – or anywhere else.

As the American journalist Dorothy Thompson wrote in her 1938 book *Refugees: Anarchy or Organization?*, "It's a fantastic commentary on the inhumanity of our times that for thousands and thousands of people a piece of paper with a stamp on it is the difference between life and death."

But before it all had started, there were other days in Holland, nicer and more memorable days, such as going with Vader (Father) to his tiny midtown office and to the public library that was beside his office to get a book by Robert Louis Stevenson. *Treasure Island* was quite popular and similar to the books Moeder bought me to read during the long wintry Friday evenings.

I remember a fine spring day – I must have been nine years old – when I was walking home with my father from his office. We passed the fish market on the Koningsplein, where people stood or sat at wooden tables eating raw herring dipped in onions. Vader had stopped walking and said to me, "Wait here a moment, I want to buy some herring for Moeder."

While I waited, I was mesmerized watching a group of men and women eating the herring. Holding the fish, called *maatjesharing*, by its tail, they would throw their heads back and slide the fish into their mouths. I could see their Adam's apples bob up and down as they swallowed the herring, and I thought to myself, *Oh, my God, ugh.* I hated the smell of this raw fish, but *maatjes* herring was (and still is) hugely popular in the Netherlands.

I recall when I was six or seven going with Vader and my brothers to the Lekstraat Synagoge on Saturday nights to daven the evening service (only later would I be old enough to go to Sabbath services on Friday nights, and to the youth minyan on Shabbat morning), walking with them down the quiet streets in the falling dusk listening to their grown-up talk. Inside the high-ceilinged hall, I would listen in awe to the beautiful tenor voice of the cantor singing the evening prayer.

On Yom Kippur, the holiest day of the year, we'd go to another synagogue in a middle-class section of town. During prayer break, while playing outdoors with my buddies, I would stop and listen to the elderly Jews who sat outside in the warm September sunshine on wooden benches in front of the synagogue reminiscing in Yiddish (which I could hardly understand) about the good old days in Mother Russia or Poland, where they had lived before the Nazis came to their country and they had to flee.

One of my favorite memories is of summer vacation. My family would go to the popular beach resort Zandvoort, about twenty-five miles (38 km) west of Amsterdam. Grateful to be away from school and homework, we enjoyed carefree days sitting in beach chairs basking in the sun or walking across the warm sand, firm under our bare feet, wading into the foaming North Sea. We'd swim through the cold water to the raft, climb up on it and sit dripping wet, the raft bobbing up and down as the waves kept rolling in. Listening to the splashing water and watching the shore and the promenade with the cafés and the crowd sitting in chairs under the trees was so relaxing.

We would take cheerful motorboat rides, stroll along the wide boulevards, and watch the restaurant tables fill up in the summer nights. We were just a family that was happy to be together enjoying carefree days. And who can forget the colorful fireworks at night? We'd gaze with loud oohs and aahs as the rockets exploded in the night sky, watching them whish and burst as the sky lit up with images in orange and white of Queen Wilhelmina and of children dancing in a circle. The crowd whooped and clapped their hands while we kids stood there gaping as it all floated away in the night summer breeze.

I remember once on a hot day when I got back from school, there was a sparkling new bike leaning against the gray brick of our apartment building. Vader had bought it. It was a big occasion. Buying a bike at that time was like buying an automobile in the postwar years. My two brothers and I stood there eyeing the bike excitedly. It was a beautiful bicycle, a gorgeous black steel frame city bike with nice flat steel handlebars.

Vader had gone to the bike store with Moeder several times and decided to buy it. He needed it for the business. After that, I recall my brothers Eli and Josef taking me for rides along the quiet back streets of residential Amsterdam, where it was safe, riding confidently in circles while I sat on the back of the bike, enjoying the ride immensely.

In prewar Holland, almost everyone got around on bicycles. You could see entire Dutch families out riding, solo or tandem. Even the queen would publicly ride a bike to the royal palace in Amsterdam.

But then the shadows of a ravaging war with Germany gathered over the country.

TWO

~

The Battle

By the time I entered fourth grade, Jews were already required to wear the yellow star.

In the spring of 1940, my family and friends took a short vacation to the pleasant town of Hilversum. We stayed at a Swiss chalet–style building, and after dinner one evening, we all took a walk. The lights in the cafes and restaurants had come on, and walking past the crowded tables, we could hear that all the talk was of war. Was a war with Nazi Germany imminent? By now the Germans had occupied Czechoslovakia and invaded Poland, Denmark, and Norway. The latest news was that Great Britain and France had declared war on Germany. Why would Germany spare the Netherlands? The Dutch military had recently mobilized, and people were clutching at straws.

There was a humming sound that hung like a cloud as a group of customers discussed the situation across the tables. Would the Germans go ahead and attack the Netherlands? Yes, that was the question, and if they did, would the Netherlands be able to ward off the attack? The Dutch Water Defense Lines – a system of dykes that could be flooded in a controlled manner – were considered to be the bulwark to ward off attacks from German forces.

"No, no," one of the guests sitting at the tables thundered, "the Germans won't attack. Of course not. They won't dare." He folded the newspaper he had been reading and slipped it into his pocket. "It would be a foolish thing to do," he went on heatedly. "The Dutch military will open up the floodgates, inundate the low-lying areas, and cut the Germans off from the rest of the country." He gave an emphatic nod. "This," he said, "will deter any attack. And don't forget," he added, "we have the Maginot Line fortifications built by France. No, no, they won't dare. Besides," he pointed out, "Germany will not violate Dutch neutrality."

Even though I was just a child (I was eight at the time), I had studied enough history to know that this sounded like the story of the young boy who stuck his finger in the hole in the dyke to forestall a flood.

Another customer seated nearby was raising his voice. "Rubbish," he shot back at them. "I'm telling you, there will be a war. The Germans could easily outflank and attack us." He glanced around the tables. "So we had better be prepared."

The following day, as we checked out of the hotel to take the train back home to Amsterdam, we heard over the radio that the Dutch forces had been put on alert.

On the night of May 10, 1940, I was awakened in the early morning darkness by the shrill noise of an air raid. I heard the throbbing, humming sound of low-flying airplanes coming closer. Then there were the distant detonations as the first bombs fell. We heard first the piercing whistle and then the thundering blasts of the bombs, followed by roaring echoes that made the windows rattle.

I lay in bed, thinking back to the people at the restaurant. As the sound of explosions got nearer, I closed my eyes and covered my ears, pulled my knees to my chest, and thought, *stop it, stop it, please*, and lay there praying we would survive the attack. God, I was scared to death. Across the room from me, my brothers were sitting up in bed, groaning, "It's the Germans." And then: *Crack boom.*

My parents tried to calm us. It took a while until the sirens and mortar shells and echoing anti-aircraft guns had subsided.

We hurried into the living room in our pajamas and sat transfixed before the radio. "In the early hours of 10 May, Germany attacked the Netherlands, Belgium, and Luxembourg. Dutch troops are blowing up bridges to slow down the German advance…"

The Netherlands was at war.

That same day, the government proclaimed a state of emergency.

In the days that followed, the country seemed to hold its breath. We stayed at home, mostly in front of the radio, listening to the nonstop reports that were coming in from all fronts. There was heavy fighting up north in Groningen, and in the south there were reports of German planes dropping parachutists near Rotterdam.

In Amsterdam, the streets were nearly deserted. Now and then a truck filled with uniformed soldiers roared by, and little groups of people stood on the street corners huddling together. It seemed people gathered together more for comfort than for news.

During those days, Vader would be sitting in his chair in a corner by the window, playing with a fountain pen. Moeder, a cup of coffee in hand, would sit down beside us in front of the radio. Nothing happened over the next few days, but I was constantly on edge, wondering when the next bombing would occur.

The schools remained closed, and we neighbor kids found ourselves looking for grenade fragments of artillery rounds that lay scattered across the streets. We would collect them and then trade the pieces among ourselves just as we had traded soccer cards.

On the third day of the war, the fighting took a turn for the worse; the front lines had collapsed, and the Dutch forces had started a full retreat. We heard Dutch radio announcers saying, "The German planes have dropped tons of bombs on the center of Rotterdam. Nazi paratroopers have landed near military fields of The Hague, the capital city. Dutch troops are withdrawing from the east front…" And the broadcasting of bad news went on and on.

THREE

IJmuiden

Our cleaning lady, a young Jewish woman, had come to our apartment with her fiancé, talking about going to IJmuiden. The town of IJmuiden had come up in the newscasts since the war had started. IJmuiden is a port city located in the north of the Netherlands.

As events unfolded, Jews as well as non-Jews were trying to flee by boat to England. Rumors were spreading that the Dutch government was providing ships for the transport of Jews to England. Our parents decided to go to the port city with my uncle's family, who lived near us. Our young cleaning lady and her fiancé would join us.

But fate had a different plan.

The following morning, while packing our bags, we heard on the radio that German Panzer divisions were advancing in the direction of Rotterdam, and Dutch forces were suffering big losses.

We hired two cabs and set out for IJmuiden. Tens of thousands of people had packed up their belongings and left the cities – especially Jews who had fled Germany earlier – all resolved to get across to England.

The distance between Amsterdam and IJmuiden was twenty-five miles (40 km), which usually was a thirty-minute drive, but with German surveillance planes swooping out of the sky and the massive flow of terrified civilians often coming to a snarling halt, it took us more than an hour. Finally we arrived at the harbor, where the quays were overcrowded with people trying to escape the Nazi onslaught.

Upon our arrival at the port, we tried to locate a ship to get us across and saw in front of us a large group of young children boarding a big passenger freighter. A young woman who had accompanied them stayed behind and waved farewell as the ship departed right before our eyes, leaving us behind ashore. This ship, the SS *Bodengraven*, was the last boat that left Holland for Great Britain. Watching the boat sailing out of the harbor was like saying goodbye to a loved one you knew you would never see again.

I remember people standing near me, exclaiming with a kind of a wail of despair, "Oh, no!" and then again, "Oh, no!" Vader and Moeder's faces showed nothing. They just stood there staring after the departing ship.

We had been so near and had missed the boat by seconds.

Afterwards, we learned that this group of Jewish children, who had been evacuated from Nazi Germany, belonged to the Kindertransport, which was organized by the Dutch and British governments and was also the work of a Christian woman named Truus Wijsmuller. She was the woman who had accompanied the children to the ship.

All around us, there was chaos. In the distance, explosions from mortars could be heard, and children were crying. We heard the anguished wails of mothers unable to soothe their terrified kids. Planes attacked a group of bicyclists. As we looked up, we saw German Heinkel and Stuka fighters passing overhead in the dark blue sky. Following a nerve-racking *boom*, we saw in the distance plumes of gray smoke shooting into the sky.

The constant rumbling of distant mortar and the rattling of gunfire scared the daylights out of me. All we wanted now was to get out of this hellhole as fast as possible.

When there was a lull in the gunfire, we started to look for a spot to sit and rest. We settled ourselves on a patch of field beneath trees and ate egg sandwiches and drank tea from the thermos bottle we had taken along. Holland's brief military resistance was over, and the future didn't look particularly bright.

From refugees who had tried to get across, we learned that Dutch outposts were now firmly in German hands.

A young uniformed Dutch soldier sitting with his back against a trunk near us, his helmet lying near his feet and his rifle leaning against the tree, was talking to us – or perhaps just to himself. He took swallows from a water bottle attached to his shoulder strap and kept repeating over and over in a monotone voice, "Yes, it's over. We have lost. Those damn Germans. We surrendered. It's over." He kept saying it again and again in a weary, apathetic, resigned voice: "It's over, all over."

So that was it, I realized with dread. Life as we knew it was over.

Night had now fallen. Our trip to Ijmuiden had been in vain. We found two cabs again and returned to Amsterdam. The landscape framed by the black sky was bleak. We passed destroyed buildings still aflame and saw many bridges blown up. Vehicles lay abandoned on the road. I felt it all in the pit of my stomach. Holland had lost, and Germany – the Nazi Germany we had fled – had won.

For a while, we were driving in silence along a road winding back and forth with trees on each side. Through the open window floated the stench of burning buildings.

"Good God," our driver muttered to the windshield. "Look at that, look at what these Germans did to us." His disturbance was met with silence. The members of my family were each brooding.

During the next two or three days, Moeder sank into a morose melancholy and stayed in bed. Vader prepared the meals, and we sat around the radio listening to the grim news. General Winkelman had signed the surrender documents on the morning of May 15, and the Dutch government and Queen Wilhelmina had fled to Great Britain, establishing a government in exile.

These were dark days. The blackout papers had disappeared from the windows, for there would be no more bombs.

We had given up the fight.

FOUR

~

Under German Control

Two weeks later, on May 29, the Germans installed a new administration headed by an Austrian Nazi named Arthur Seyss-Inquart. Now, German soldiers in uniform, rifles slung over their backs, could be seen in the streets everywhere.

There had been food rationing already before the war. Now that the Nazis had occupied the country, the rationing had become more stringent. Everyone received coupons from the distribution office (which was controlled by the Nazis) for bread, meat, sugar, shoes, and clothes.

Meanwhile, we tried to get back to normal life. My two brothers went back to Hogere Burgerschool (HBS), "higher civic school" or high school. Vader went about his daily life, I went back to elementary school, and Moeder did the usual household chores, cleaning, shopping, cooking, and helping Papa run the business. Sometimes, the entire family would sit at the table in the living room in the evenings under the lamplight, playing Scrabble, Monopoly, or a game called Don't Get Angry.

On the surface, it was business as usual.

We kept playing the outdoor games we used to play before the war. At school, we organized fights with the school on the opposite side of the quadrangle; one side, the "good guys," fought the other, the "bad guys." Whoever advanced upon and captured the good guys' side won; hence, everyone was fighting everyone, which was great fun. Admittedly, I was a willing participant. We had a fine time.

At school, I was assigned to a specific task; I was in charge of punching holes in bottle caps, then putting straws in them and handing them out. I was a terrific bottle-cap puncher.

And there were the basketball and punchball games at school. I went with school friends in the winter ice skating and in the summer bicycling (since Vader needed his bike for the business, I rented a bike), and we would stop in a field outside town and watch as rows of German soldiers marched in formation in the sun on the field. Hoarse voices counted cadence. We cursed them to hell.

"Hey," one of my friends scoffed in Dutch, "look at these sad sacks, these Nazis. Look at how clumsily they change steps." He shook his head. "Nitwits."

"Right," another sneered. "Wish they'd disappear off the face of the earth." And he spat on the ground in disgust.

And I just stood there, silent. Hearing the shouting in German, I wished I could make the entire group of soldiers disappear with a wave of my hand. I'd like to say *abracadabra*, and *poof*, off they would go.

When I went to school – it was a ten-minute walk – watching the columns of gray-clad soldiers goose-stepping through the street singing German songs sent a chill up my spine.

I went to a non-Jewish school. I recall one day sitting in the classroom listening to the teacher explaining something to us, with the background noise of a German song coming in through open windows as German soldiers marched past our building. As we sat there in silence, facing the books on our desks, the words of the song were sweeping through the room.

"*Die Fahne hoch! Die Reihen fest geschlossen! SA marschiert mit ruhig festem Schritt*" (The flag on high! The ranks tightly closed! The Sturmabteilung [Brownshirts] march with quiet, steady step).

This was our new reality. Jews were no longer equal citizens, and German soldiers were the soundtrack to our school days.

My father was very skilled with his hands and often would repair shoes in his spare time. I asked him if he could put metal spikes on the bottom of my shoes. "You know, like the spike-heeled boots the German soldiers are wearing, making that clip-clop sound walking down the streets."

He was seated at his workbench examining someone's shoe while we were talking. He considered it for a moment, gave a shrug, then putting away the shoe he was working on, he turned to me. "It's not a good idea to imitate those Nazi people." Another shrug. "I don't like the clippity-clop sound of these Nazi people. But listen, if it means that much to you, fine, I'll do it."

And sure enough, Vader managed. And I would proudly walk to school in the spike-soled shoes. I loved that staccato sound. That was the one thing I liked about these Nazi soldiers. Their boots that made the clippity-clop sound.

Then several months later, things changed.

FIVE

Persecution

Until the beginning of 1941, the German authorities had lulled us Jews into a sense of false security, didn't make themselves noticeable, were friendly and polite and sometimes would even be helpful, carrying heavy bundles to buildings for the elderly. Then came the sudden change.

In the second half of 1941, the Nazi occupation government in Holland established a Jewish council called de Joodse Raad. Its purpose was to mediate the Nazi government's orders with the Jewish community. Before the change, there was very little to negotiate. Basically life just went on. The country was placed under the Reichskommissariat, a German civilian government headquartered in The Hague, and German military forces were stationed at bases in different localities.

But then the rules got more stringent for the Jews; every month, a tsunami of new regulations and measures was announced. Signs reading "Prohibited for Jews" appeared.

Then as though it were a reflex response, in February 1941, the first strike occurred. A vicious fight broke out in an Amsterdam café between Dutch Jews and the occupying German police. One day later, four hundred random young people, all Jews, were arrested, transported by train to Germany, and disappeared. The brutal arrest and disappearance outraged the population, and a general strike in Amsterdam was proclaimed; dockworkers in the city walked off the job; some 300,000 workers joined the strike, and there were no streetcars or buses. Shops closed in solidarity. Other Dutch cities joined in. The stakes got higher. Clashes with Dutch Nazis left nine Jewish citizens dead and many wounded.

A Nazi response was not long in coming; the strikes were brutally suppressed. By sundown, the Germans – assisted by armed Nationaal Socialistische Beweging (NSB) people (Dutch Nazi collaborators) – temporarily closed off the Jewish neighborhood. Trucks pulled up in front of apartment buildings, and more Jewish men were rounded up, beaten, and taken away, forcing the Dutch population back to work.

Anti-Jewish restrictions were tightened up: bank accounts were blocked; Jewish Dutch citizens were allowed for private use only 250 guilders ($455 US dollars) a month and were ordered to have a red identifying letter *J* stamped in their passports; every Jew in Holland had to register at the offices of the new German administration – including half Jews with one Jewish grandparent. (This data would help the Nazis later on to round up Jews and send them to Nazi extermination camps.) The Jews were prohibited from pools and parks, and children from public schools.

Then in May 1942, like a thunderclap out of the blue, the most humiliating order was issued (or we thought at the time it was the most humiliating; we would learn much about humiliation as time went on): Jews were required to wear the yellow Star of David on their outer clothes. That decree was passed to us, as all the rules were, by the Joodse Raad (Jewish Council). It was followed by notification that we were no longer invited to attend entertainment events or soccer championship games. This was a bucket of cold water. The new decree seemed to proclaim: *Jews! Go away! All of you. You are not wanted here!* It was like a punch in the gut. *You are different from us. You are an outsider. You don't belong here. You are not one of us. Go away!*

I was confused. Remember, I was a child, just ten years old. I had no idea that my world could be devastated by an army dressed in gray who goose-stepped and clickity-clacked. These men could really issue orders that we had to follow? I didn't know what to think. But I knew the adults around me were frightened.

Lord. It was a pretty awful sight, watching mother sitting there at home in her armchair nervously sewing the yellow star on our clothes. Each Dutch Jewish resident from age six and up was required to wear the star given to us by the Jewish Council on our outer clothing. At home, we kept silent, we didn't talk much, but Moeder's face spoke volumes. The emotions inside her must have been whirling. I did not yet know the meaning of the word *anxiety*, but it was spelled out on my mother's face.

Vader, too, hardly spoke a word. Haggard-faced, he went about his business. My two brothers continued going to the HBS, and I walked each day to school.

The first time I laid eyes on that yellow star was unsettling. The sight of the yellow star with the black letters *JOOD* in the center of it was disturbing; I felt like now I was a hunted animal, a target. I was fair game, a very uncomfortable feeling. Nonetheless, I continued playing with my non-Jewish friends like before. It made me feel confident, because they never acknowledged the star.

In hindsight, I realize I did not know what conversation went on behind my back; were they talking about me at home? Did their parents object to them playing with me? Subconsciously, an uneasy feeling had started hanging around me. The Nazis had prevailed with their star, because I did feel like I was somebody different.

Deep down I felt violated, molested. It was a sense of indignation and humiliation. I felt as if I had been stripped naked in the street in full view of the world. When I first put on my coat with the disgusting star on it, automatically my eyes lowered from shame and embarrassment. I wanted to walk down the street, curious to know how people would react. The Dutch people – my neighbors whom I saw every day – would they see me the way I was seeing me?

The truth was, they hardly looked up, didn't seem to care (which was a relief), and when I caught someone casting a quick, guarded glance at me and then looking away, that was okay. Over time I learned to put up with it, live with it. The star became part of my life, like eating and sleeping.

The first day back at school wearing the yellow star taught me much about my people. As I entered the classroom, a group of girls and boys were laughing and talking together. Suddenly the room fell silent. One of my friends was glancing up, nudged his friend who sat beside him, and both stared as though hypnotized by the yellow star. Then quickly, almost guiltily, they looked away. Soon angry murmurs of protests could be heard: If the Nazis were so unfeeling and inhuman, they would pay a price.

I was astonished hearing them talk this way about the Germans and how the NSB, the Dutch Nazis, behaved toward the Jews. I was awash in total gratitude. Perhaps the Nazis' attempt at humiliating the Jews would not work. But I was shy by nature, and the whole class was looking at me. The entire scene was all about me. I did not want to blow it out of proportion. So I just sat down, nodded, smiled, and kept silent.

When class was over and the bell rang, I was the first one to walk out the door.

In the corridor, my soccer team buddy Guus Peters stopped me. His tone was casual. "Our game," he said, "tomorrow six o'clock." He looked at me searchingly. "All right?"

"Sure." I nodded and then mumbled, "All right."

"Right." Guus smiled broadly and patted me on the shoulder. "See you later."

Filled with a feeling close to love, I watched him turn and walk away.

A month later, new orders were issued. A curfew for Jews was imposed: between the hours of eight p.m. and six a.m., we were to remain at home. The new state of the country was frightening. My family was very lucky. In 1942, an uncle of mine (my mother's brother) in Switzerland had managed to acquire Paraguayan passports for us.

Anyone who held a passport to any Latin American country was assured protection from deportation to Nazi extermination camps and would be sent to internment camps instead to be exchanged by the Nazis for Germans held in captivity.

More and more Jewish men were sent to labor camps in the Netherlands, creating the initial impression that they wouldn't be sent to any feared concentration camps, because they had already been put to work in the Netherlands.

In July 1942, the Nazis began transporting the first Jews to Westerbork, a transit camp in the northeast of the Netherlands. At the same time, the occupation officials announced that Dutch Jews failing to comply with orders to report to German labor camps would be dealt with by the Gestapo. As the transports began to roll, the Dutch police actively collaborated and assisted the German authorities in rounding up Jews on the streets and in their homes.

One morning, a Jewish neighbor family was taken in. I had witnessed the raid, as Dutch policemen arrived in a police truck and took them away. A couple of days later, standing by the rear window, looking out at the other side of the corner building, I saw a young man in shirt sleeves descending a rope hand over hand, then lowering himself onto the missing neighbors' balcony. He broke a window and climbed into the vacant apartment. Soon he reappeared with dinnerware in his hands and put it into a large woven basket attached to another rope, which was then hauled up by his family members to their fifth-floor apartment. They were Dutch fascists. In this way, they had robbed the apartment of many valuables.

We figured we had better not call the police. We said nothing.

And the transports kept rolling.

In those dark times, the official radio programming in the Netherlands was under German control, glorifying the offensive warfare of Nazi Germany's early military successes.

As columns of Nazi soldiers marched along the streets, my parents sat listening to the latest war bulletins from the clandestine BBC radio, being careful not to get caught by the Gestapo. People who got caught listening were immediately shipped off to the so-called labor camps.

We felt desperate.

Jews were now no longer safe in the Netherlands and had to get out.

But how could we escape?

My parents considered the options.

My brothers and I would stand behind closed doors eavesdropping as Vader and Moeder discussed in low voices the possibility of fleeing Nazi-occupied Holland. The consequences of getting caught were to be shipped off to the so-called labor camps.

One idea was that Vader would try to cross the border into Switzerland (with a smuggler who'd been recommended), and if everything went well, he would send us a coded message to follow him. But Moeder fiercely objected to the plan, pointing out that the "recommended" smuggler might leave us stranded at the border, or worse, hand us over to the Gestapo, after he collected his money. What then? Moeder's voice rose at the very thought of what might happen to us. No, no, she told Vader firmly, she was dead set against the plan. It was too risky, too dangerous.

In July 1942, rumors buzzed around town that the Gestapo had obtained direct orders from the Reich Security Main Office in Berlin to round up all Latin American passport holders and deport them to the camps in the east.

As mentioned, these documents were supposed to be a key to freedom, to help protect the holder from getting rounded up. But in reality, quite the reverse took place.

SIX

Departure

The two men who came for us arrived on bicycles. They had been sent to the upscale, southern section of Amsterdam carrying the list of "exchange Jews" – people who could be used to negotiate for German prisoners of war.

They came on a Wednesday morning in September 1942, at nine a.m. We were literally about to go into hiding. My father had spoken to a business friend he worked with who was willing to help get us get to someplace safe. The woman had arrived a few minutes earlier to take us to the hiding place, a safe house in Groningen in North Holland.

We had always anticipated with dread those knocks on the door. When they came, the knocks were loud, and an authoritative voice called out in Dutch, "*Politie, open de deur!*" (This is the police. Open up!).

Moeder, turning pale, exchanged a quick glance with Vader.

The voice called out again: "Open up in there!"

Vader motioned her to the door.

Moeder opened it, and standing there were two tough-looking Dutch Nazi plainclothes policemen.

Unbidden, they made their way inside, glanced around the room, and ordered us in steely voices to pack our belongings and come with them to an assembly point, a neo-Renaissance municipal theater building called the Hollandsche Schouwburg, located in the center of Amsterdam.

As I turned to look at Vader, I could see a sudden tension flicker across his face as one of the policeman took out a list (signed by the Gestapo) with our names on it. Standing close to the men, I could see the writing: there was Vader's name, Ephraim Wigdor Holles; Moeder's name, Regina Rachel Holles; my two brothers' names, Elias and Joseph; and my name, Wolf. One of the policemen callously thrust it under Moeder's nose. She stared at the names wide-eyed. The officer nodded toward the woman standing there a few paces away and barked, "Who's that?"

Moeder kept her voice casual. "She's the cleaning lady."

The policeman studied her for a moment, glanced at the list, and shrugged. Before he could say anything, the woman slipped out the door. At that moment, Vader looked across at me and whispered, "Weep, son. Weep loudly."

On command, I began to cry, but once the tears were unleashed, I soon began to weep with genuine, gulping sobs. My two brothers, disconcerted, stared at me.

"Stop it!" the officer named Kuiper snapped, looking at me. "Shut up, kid."

I saw the expression on the other policeman's face soften. Officer Bakker took his partner aside and spoke in a low voice. "Maybe we should let them go?"

"No way." Kuiper's voice hardened. "We can't."

While the policemen were momentarily distracted by this discussion, I saw Vader rush out the door to the building's staircase, from which he managed to escape across the roof.

We would later find out that he worked hard to avoid our deportation. But for the moment, I stood there perplexed, filled with fear. I looked over at Moeder but didn't say a word.

I was just a child and still processing, trying to figure the world out. In the world I was living in, people were here one day and gone the next. I knew we were at war – mostly because food was rationed. I knew we were Jews and considered peculiar, though I did not know why. And now, when my father slipped out the door, I suddenly became aware that his life might be in grave danger. These people might kill him.

Officer Bakker must have noticed something, because he glanced around, then stared across at Moeder and snarled, "Where is your husband?"

Moeder gave a shrug and said nothing.

Officer Kuiper turned to her and snarled, "You heard him. Where is your husband?"

Moeder kept quiet, but she and my brothers looked startled when they realized that Vader was actually gone.

Bakker turned to Kuiper and motioned with his head toward the door. Kuiper nodded and strode out of the room, searched the three-room apartment, and came back growling grimly, "*Verdomme* – damn – he is not here." And to Moeder: "You have twenty minutes to pack your things."

"Oh, dear Lord," Moeder murmured. Furtively wiping her eyes with the palms of her hands, she started bustling about, gathering essential belongings, while the Dutch officers stood there looking on.

Bakker was guarding the front door. Kuiper, casually whistling a Dutch song, wandered into the kitchen. He pulled open the top drawer of our kitchen cupboards, glanced inside, gave his companion a conspiratorial wink, and reached for half a dozen raw eggs stored in an egg carton. He tipped his head back and cracked them open one by one directly into his mouth.

I watched him in horrified fascination as the bile rose into my throat.

Distraught, Moeder packed things for an unknown period of time. Packing for summer and winter? How long would we be gone? Who's to say? Who knew? We helped her, putting stacks of clothing in the suitcases.

When we had finished and were about to leave the apartment, Officer Kuiper looked at Moeder and held out his hand. "The keys, please," he demanded, piercing her with a cold glare.

Moeder meekly handed the house and street door keys over. In all likelihood, once we were shipped off to the camps, the Reichskommissariat (civilian occupation regime) would give the two men official permission to rob our apartment of all valuables.

I was worried about Vader. What had happened to him? It was nearly impossible to escape when the Nazi collaborators were on the scene. During raids, the *moffen* (the Dutch name for the NSB, the Nazi collaborators) would stand there at both ends of the street, their carbines at the ready, sending the ominous signals: *No way, people! Don't even think about it!*

After we had been arrested, we were escorted by the two Dutch policemen out the door into the street and onto the streetcar like criminals to be put in prison. People who surrounded us could clearly see the yellow stars sewn on our outer clothes and the two Dutch policemen escorting us. They knew what was going to happen to us. Yet they stared noncommittally at us and turned their faces away as if we were not human.

What on earth had we done wrong to be forced out of our homes? What had we done that these people wouldn't even look at us?

The moment they came for us and we boarded that streetcar, I felt I was caught in a nightmare, trapped in a hostile world. My family had been deprived of our home, our belongings, and our freedom. I could not know then that this wound would torture me for most of my life, and I am lucky to be able to tell of this experience, lucky to be alive and sane. Why I survived, only God knows.

We now were officially declared prisoners and would be deported to God only knew what horrible place. Moeder was admirably calm and silent all the way across town to the assembly point. None of the passengers seated next to us in the streetcar would reach out or say a friendly, encouraging word. Not one of them.

The majority of the Dutch population had stayed passive and remained silent in the early years of the occupation. Any form of resistance to the Nazi occupation took time to evolve. But it must be said that there was a growing number of Dutch people who risked their lives saving Jews by hiding them in their homes during the war. More aggravating was the way the institutions responded. The police and civil service willingly cooperated with the Nazi agenda. Nederlandse Spoorwegen, the Dutch railway company, would eventually be forced to pay compensation to those who were deported to concentration camps on the trains it cheerfully organized, at a profit.

The roundups and deportations were usually executed in a dispassionate and methodical manner. The two Dutch policemen who arrested us were totally passionless, hard-hearted beings, showing no more compassion than a statue carved from stone.

The point of departure was the Hollandsche Schouwburg, a squat, angular three-story stone building with a dark gray façade. It was a large municipal theater that had sometimes been designated for Jewish occasions and festivities and was therefore appropriated by the Nazis. It was there that we remained for an entire week until the Nazis had enough people rounded up, and then we were transported in ordinary passenger trains to Westerbork, a transit camp in the northern part of Holland.

The grueling wait of seven long days and nights in that overcrowded, devastatingly depressing theater felt like an eternity. It seemed to go on and on. I kept wondering what had happened to Vader. Where was he? Was he safe? Moeder wasn't a big help either. I couldn't know how frightened she was, since she tried to hold herself together for our sake and didn't say anything. She just sat, downcast and hollow-eyed, with a dispirited expression on her haggard face.

Watching her, I wondered what thoughts were running through her mind. Being without her husband, taken from her home in broad daylight, not knowing what the future held. I was frightened too, but no one was depending on me. She had my brothers and me looking to her for support, and there she was, the only parent left to deal with an unthinkable future. My mind was clouded with worry. But I could still see and feel my mother's fear, knowing at the same time that she was trying to be brave for us.

Most of the time we spent wandering the auditorium or sitting and sleeping in the brick-red plush theater seats. During the day, Dutch nurses, who worked for the Jewish Council, passed out meals and drinks. Kids ran up and down the aisles. Mothers tried to calm their crying babies. From where I sat, glancing around, I saw no one I could talk to, no boys I knew, just more and more families sitting there, waiting.

A growing number of people poured in. The smell of hot coffee, sweat, and traces of perfume lingered for all the days we were in the auditorium. The air was thick with a sharp, almost tangy odor. I supposed it was the smell of fear, of the tension of not knowing what lay in store for us. Here and there, an elderly person fainted away and was rushed on a gurney down the hallway to a makeshift hospital ward on the ground floor.

Late in the evenings (and sometimes in the nights), uniformed German soldiers would strut about on stage and bellow German expletives at us in brutal voices. I couldn't understand them, but their screaming would send cold shivers through me, and automatically I would clap my hands over my ears to block those coarse profanities.

One of the ways these monsters delighted in entertaining themselves was by ordering women on stage and forcing them to sing a song while standing on one foot.

One evening, one of the SS glanced about and picked a young, blond woman who was seated nearby, gesturing for her to come on stage.

Beneath the stage lights, the terror in the woman's eyes was evident as she stood there on one foot on the podium and began to sing a Dutch folk song: "*Daar bij die molen, die mooie molen…*" (Oh, there at the mill, that beautiful mill…).

As she stood, trying hard to keep her balance, her shaking voice faltered. One of the Nazi louts standing near her gave her a brutal shove from behind that sent her flying across the stage floor.

Fellow Nazi guards who stood nearby broke out into ribald laughter. The young woman lay there for a moment, shocked, gasping for breath. Then she scrambled to her feet, ran back to her seat, and burying her face in her hands, burst into tears.

By this time, the theater had become a crowded mass of people, all wearing the yellow star on their clothing.

Finally, on the seventh day, the SS ordered us over the loudspeaker to head for the exit and get ready for departure. Now what seemed like endless groups of worn-down families – parents carrying babies or holding the hands of their little frightened kids – started shuffling toward the arched exits, thankful to escape the oppressively stifling air.

That Monday, September 28, 1942, was a chilly autumn day. Many people had gathered to watch us climb into local buses while Dutch Nazi officers stood there with automatic weapons impatiently ordering us to move along. "*Verdergaan, mensen!* Keep going, people! Move along!" they ordered. "Clear the way! Clear the way!"

Minutes later, we boarded the buses and were on our way to the old Gothic-style Centraal railroad station, where a passenger train was waiting for us.

The unknown filled us with fear.

What was awaiting us out there?

SEVEN

~

Westerbork

On a Tuesday morning, September 29, 1942, our train pulled into the small railway platform of the transit camp Westerbork.

Westerbork was surrounded by forest grounds and looked deceptively bucolic. The green and brown colors of the trees hid the camp's watch towers and layers of barbed wire. Later I would learn that we were situated in the middle of the eastern province Drente, about eighty miles (130 km) north of Amsterdam.

During the ride across the Dutch countryside, Moeder had barely spoken a word, just sitting motionless, staring with dull eyes out the window at the changing Dutch landscape sliding past us: brown stone windmills at the edge of stream beds, large patches of birch forests, little green meadows with grazing cattle, and brightly colored flower fields alternating with ditches crisscrossing flat farmlands. We did not ordinarily drive out of the city, and the countryside might have been beautiful scenery for me. But my father's absence – and what it was doing to Moeder – took away all my spirit.

All three of us tried to get her attention, to do something to pull her out of her trance-like state. The black uniformed Marechaussee, the Military Police, were guarding the train. We were grateful they were Dutch and not Germans. Unlike the Dutch police, the Military Police were neutral and friendly, and we considered them as being on our side.

At the camp, men and women were segregated and lived in different quarters, but were allowed to mingle freely during the day. Children up to the age of twelve were placed in the women's barracks. Being just ten myself, I was placed with Moeder.

During the first few months, my mother and I lived in a tiny rectangular room in a small cottage looking out at barbed-wire fences and watchtowers. My brothers lived in the men's barracks. Several months later, my mother and I were transferred to the oblong barracks located across the railroad station, housing about two hundred people.

Besides being imprisoned and robbed of our human rights, it needs to be said that life in Westerbork was tolerable up to a certain point and was not like what you would call a "tough" concentration camp. We got enough food and were treated fairly.

We seldom saw the dreaded SS with the grisly skull-and-crossbones insignias that were on their gray-green hats. The compound itself was run by members of a Jewish council made up of Jewish elders, the majority of whom were German Jews who had been in the camp from the very beginning. The camp was guarded by the Marechaussee.

There was a pharmacy, a hospital with doctors, a dental clinic, a hairdresser, and the police (not very popular) with "OD" badges (standing for *Ordnungsdiest*, order maintenance) pinned to their left breast pockets. My brothers and I enjoyed sport-filled days with soccer games. There was also entertainment – cabaret and theater performances with German and Dutch Jewish inmates who were top performers with broad professional theater experience. Every Monday night, there was a Bunte Abend, an "enjoyable evening" to distract the inmates from the dreadful transports of the next morning. Later we would learn that all of these events and services were staged to maintain a sense of calm among the Jewish prisoners and give them a false sense of normalcy and hope of survival.

But fear was never far away, a shadow following every move. We worried about the days that lay ahead of us.

Around mid-July 1943, a group of six hundred prisoners – including us – was briefly transferred to Kamp Amersfoort, a concentration camp in central Holland. We were held there briefly to make room for an influx of new arrivals in Westerbork.

We arrived on a balmy summer afternoon and marched two miles southward (with Dutch police escort) to the camp. The place reminded us of a peaceful resort surrounded by a thick birch tree forest. But we had an uncomfortable feeling that this image was deceiving and there was more to it than a peaceful quiet. We lived in tolerable conditions similar to Westerbork. Later it became known that the place was a temporary transit camp from 1942 to 1943 from where prisoners were sent to Buchenwald and Mauthausen. We lived for thirty days in makeshift brick and stone barracks and slept in narrow iron frame beds arranged in double tiers.

The days passed, and we tried not to think. After the short stay, we were shipped back to Westerbork in early August.

Uppermost in people's minds was the war. How long would it last? Was it going to be one or two or three years, maybe more? Nobody knew. In the meantime, the mantra in the camp was "Hang in there" or "Don't let your heads hang down."

That was the beginning.

But soon the darkness was closing in on us, and things began to change.

The deportation from Westerbork to the concentration camps in Germany and Poland began to roll. With growing fear, we watched as the passenger cars arriving at the camp were replaced by freight cars, and uniformed SS men disembarked.

I well remember when the train with the metal train sign "WESTERBORK-AUSCHWITZ – AUSCHWITZ-WESTERBORK" pulled in. The cars were emptied out by a cleaning crew of inmates, going from car to car, cleaning the buckets used for toilets and picking up garbage and litter from the floor.

The cleaning crew in Westerbork discovered concealed messages scribbled on little scraps of paper they found hidden in the cracks across floors and wood benches of train cars. These notes described the hideous conditions of camps at Auschwitz and Sobibor. They told of the horror that was happening there, of the gas ovens and the extermination of hundreds of prisoners. Apparently these were put there by the "cleaning work unit" of prisoners at Auschwitz who cleaned the train cars that would return to Westerbork. As this information was shared secretly throughout the camp, our fear increased. Who would be next?

And today, many years later, as I'm sitting here writing this, it seems surreal to me that despite all this, despite the fact that the Dutch Jews in Westerbork knew by then what was happening once they were put on the deportation list and were going to be shipped off to extermination camps, we didn't resist and try to escape but instead stayed in denial and tried to dismiss the unbelievable monstrosity. Like ostriches with their heads buried in the sand.

But then what else could we possibly have done? Rebel? Fight the armed SS guards? Try to flee? Many of us tried these things. But those willing to fight were too few, and anyone who tried to leave his assigned place was shot by the SS on the spot. We had witnessed this, the ruthless killing and lack of humanity in these creatures sent to make sure we stayed where we were told and followed every order. Bit by bit the Nazis groomed us to accept one wretched change in our lives after the other, each change a step lower down the abyss, until those passengers willingly walked onto the train knowing where they were headed. They had nowhere else to go.

Until we stepped up to that train, ignoring reality was our only option.

These Auschwitz inmates leaving warning notes for the next group of passengers that were going to be in the same situation, as I can see now, were both courageous and desperate. They at least tried to save whoever came behind.

On days before the train came to deliver people, and sometimes randomly on other nights in the summer, the prisoners played accordions. The evening air was mild and the notes were rising high, hovering over the heads of dancing couples, prisoners who for those few minutes were unconcerned about their future. They were moving around to the beat of the refreshing Dutch folk songs – really a touching moment. Auschwitz be damned, they wanted to live and enjoy life as long they could, and to hell with the SS and with Nazi Germany. And uncaring Europe.

When the cabaret performances were held every week, we young-sters would nimbly climb up the wooden support beams underneath the slanting roof of the barracks and watch the performances from high up as though they were the orchestra seats with the best viewing angle. In hindsight, I keep wondering how people who knew exactly what lay in store for them could burst into mirthful laughter and merrily dance to cheerful music. How was it possible?

Maybe many thought it was all a lie, and they did not believe that people could do such horrible things to each other? Maybe the Nazis would put us in labor camps and would "resettle" us (the Nazis' term) and relocate us to the east? Maybe the conditions of life would be the same in the other camps? Heck, maybe the war would be over soon and everything would be just fine?

Maybe, maybe not.

But every Tuesday, the brutal reality would set in. The dreadful day of the deportations arrived.

EIGHT

~

Tuesdays

Every Tuesday, starting in July 1942 and running until September 1944, transports left Westerbork for Auschwitz at about eleven in the morning.

The greatly feared transport list made its appearance on Tuesday. Everyone fervently hoped not to be on it.

Generally, on Tuesday, around four a.m., a member of the Jewish police force (OD) came into the sleeping women's and men's barracks, the lights went on, and everyone startled awake. The OD person glanced around, climbed onto a chair, and began to read impassively beneath the overhead lights the names (which the OD themselves had picked) of prisoners that had been selected for deportation. I remember sitting there and listening to the names, my heart pounding in my throat, thinking, will we be next in line?

After a few moments, the call-up started:

"Lea Sternberg…"

A shocked voice replied: "*Ja*, yes."

"Saul and Ruth Wagenaar…"

Another surprised female voice: "Yes."

"Sarah Koopman…"

"*Ja*," a voice came back.

The woman stood there and wiped her eyes.

We watched helplessly as our fellow inmates got the bad news.

The call-up usually lasted thirty minutes. Then the lights dimmed somewhat and the police left.

Those called up would hug friends and relatives.

There was a lot of crying and sobbing.

We, the lucky ones holding South American papers, were for the time being exempt from deportation and would stare wooden-faced at them as they began to pack their things.

As it became known what awaited them, everyone who had the chance would do anything to get off these fearful lists. Some would bribe officials, offering their wedding rings, expensive jewelry, their bracelets, watches, and gemstones, and sometimes girls would go so far as to offer their young bodies if it would gain their exemption.

If you were fortunate enough to find a doctor who would get you on the sick list and into the hospital ward, you would be barred from getting on a transport. Others tried and succeeded in joining the OD and so could delay the transport to the east for another couple of weeks. But in the end, almost everybody would be shipped off to the extermination camps located in Poland, to Auschwitz, Treblinka, and Sobibor, or to Bergen-Belsen in East Germany.

About a month after the transports began, we were reunited with Vader at Westerbork. He had gotten picked up during a razzia (a police roundup) in the southern part of Amsterdam and was sent on a penal transport to Westerbork, where he was placed in the punishment barracks, called the Penal Block. He wore a white *S* on his jacket designating him for punishment. But he soon got released from the Penal Block because of the Paraguayan papers, which gave him the preferential status of an "exchange" Jew.

He found us in one of the long wooden barracks. We ran to him and we all hugged.

"What happened to you?"

"I was at my friend's house, trying to arrange our escape. It came to nothing," he began. "When I found out that you were taken away by the police,

I spent the first night in the small hotel near the Heerengracht Museum on a quiet street." He turned to Moeder. "Remember the museum?"

"Yes," Moeder said, looking at the four of us. "We often spent time together there."

"The following evening, I returned to our apartment. I waited for any sign of the police. It was clear, so I unlocked the door with the key I still had and went inside."

Moeder stared at him, disbelieving. "You went back to our apartment?"

"Yes."

"The police might have come back."

"They didn't. I stayed there for several weeks."

Ma's brow furrowed. "What about the neighbors? Didn't they see you?"

"I kept an eye out. I avoided everyone and only went out at night. I know one of the police officers at the Hoofdbureau," he said, referencing the police headquarters. "He said he would warn me if any cop went to the apartment." He paused a moment. "When I learned that you were deported to Westerbork, I sent food parcels whenever possible." He paused again. "When I shopped for the parcels, I didn't dare wear the yellow star lest I be detected.

"In short, my friend at the Hoofdbureau lied. A couple of days ago, the police surrounded our street and started banging on doors. I was walking to the house. As soon as I saw them, I tried to run, but they caught me. They arrested me for not wearing the star and put me on the train to Westerbork as a *Sträfling*." That was a prisoner. He let out a deep breath and showed us the white *S* on his jacket. "They released me earlier today. Thank God I found you."

Moeder broke into a broad smile. We watched as she hugged Vader, happy to have him back.

On Tuesdays, during the day of deportation, there was a curfew until the prisoners were on board. People stayed inside the barracks and watched through the windows what was happening.

We could see the long line of rusty brown cattle cars standing at the empty railroad waiting for these hapless prisoners to come struggling up the narrow platform with their paltry belongings: a rolled-up blanket, a suitcase, or a bread bag dangling down their backs.

Soon, around ten a.m., we saw the first people emerge from the barracks: little frightened children holding onto their mother's or father's hands, young women soothing crying babies as they headed toward the waiting train. The policemen walked alongside them, calling out: "*Doorlopen!* Move along! Move along! Keep it moving!"

Invalids were being wheeled or carried on stretchers by the OD people to the waiting cattle cars.

Prior to departure, SS officers gathered on the platform to check the lists, making sure that everyone was on the train. They stood there looking on impassively from the platform as families were pushing their way into the cattle cars, trying desperately to stick together.

Around eleven a.m., when all was settled, the train driver motioned to the SS, climbed up into the locomotive, blew the whistle, and the train started moving.

The SS men, rifles slung over their backs, swung up and closed the doors behind them while then commandant SS Obersturmführer Gemmeker stood on the platform in his brown leather overcoat and riding breeches next to his little dog, watched stolidly as the train pulled out, heading eastward toward the death camps.

After the curfew, I recall seeing prisoners standing behind the cattle cars' small barred windows waving goodbye to relatives and friends who stood there on the platform watching the windows of the train cars go by.

I remember one young, good-looking woman. Her husband was about to board the train to Auschwitz alone. He had put his arm around her as she began to cry. As he stood there comforting her, she kept shaking her head from side to side, trying hard not to cry. He told her that everything would be fine. They would see each other again soon, and maybe in a camp similar to Westerbork. Yes, everybody tried to make the best of a hopeless situation. After the curfew, I saw her standing on the platform sobbing hysterically, tears streaming from her eyes as the train left the station. I never saw them again.

And still, I find myself wondering what these SS officers overseeing the deportation at that railroad station were thinking. Perhaps they weren't even thinking about where the prisoners were ending up. Maybe they didn't care. What did they tell their wives about how they spent their days, and how could they face their children back home?

But then you might ask yourself, if they did care, so what? If they knew (and of course they knew) what was going to happen to the deportees, what could they have done? Disobey orders?

Time and again, when being confronted with the monstrosities of the Holocaust, former SS troops would shake their heads in mute denial, shrug their shoulders, and claim flat-eyed, *we didn't know, had no idea*. But then what could a single Nazi officer have done? Refuse his superior officer's orders and face the bullet?

PART TWO

Bergen-Belsen

NINE

Next Stop

January 11, 1944, daybreak. We were next in line now.

Our names had been checked off, and we were put on the transport list to the Bergen-Belsen concentration camp.

We started off at Westerbork as a group of over one thousand people, boarded a regular passenger train, and traveled through a seemingly unending long night through hostile German countryside. We made one stop, at a dark, deserted railroad station in Bremen. When we arrived, there wasn't a soul in sight; we saw only a couple of steel-helmeted SS soldiers, rifles slung on their backs, pacing the empty platform.

A German voice was booming out across the empty platforms: "*Das Betreten des Bahnhof-Areal ist verboten*" (Entry to the railway station is forbidden to the public).

Looking out the window at the bleak, empty station in front of us, the passengers in our compartment figured that the reason must have been because of us passing through.

We arrived at Bergen-Belsen on a cold, wet, dreary wintry day after a train ride of about ten hours and were ordered to debark from the train at a narrow loading platform in the middle of nowhere surrounded by a sea of gray, wintry farmland.

Machine gun–toting Waffen SS with growling German shepherds straining on leashes herded us onto waiting military trucks, and after driving twenty minutes in silence through the snow-covered Lühneburg Heath, we reached the desolate-looking Bergen-Belsen camp.

My first impression of the camp was chilling. I felt my chest-tighten.

We found ourselves looking at long rows of low-roofed wooden barracks and about a thirteen-foot-high electrically charged barbed-wire fence with coils of concertina wire along its top encircling the place.

Menacing-looking wooden lookout towers sat at intervals of about thirty meters and were manned by SS soldiers who watched the camp through high-powered binoculars. As we stared at the chilling sight spread out before us, it seemed as if the gloating devil itself was sneeringly welcoming us inside.

We took all this in as we debarked from the trucks. Under a hail of abusive SS yelling and dog barking, we were led like a flock of lambs through the barbed-wire gates.

Male and female prisoners were separated.

The fifty-meter-long filthy barracks had hardwood plank flooring and plywood tables with wooden benches set in the middle between the two rows of three-tiered bunk beds. After we waited for maybe thirty minutes inside the dimly lit empty barracks building with small windows on both sides, Blockältesten (who had been picked by the SS and were in charge of barracks assignments) handed us a slice of bread with a scoop of soft white cheese on top and informed us of our barracks number and bunk beds; ours was number five, where my father was given the bottom and me the middle bunk. My brothers' barracks were located in a different section of the camp; my mother was in the women's barracks.

There was one medium-sized toilet stall in each barracks building, and attached was a bare lavatory with cast iron wash basins. Outside, about a hundred yards from the first barracks, stood a large, doorless wooden shack, the camp's outdoor latrine.

Mr. Weiss – the head of barracks number five – who led us to our new quarters, told us that in the mornings we would be expected to convene at the Appellplatz, a large, open roll-call ground located in the center of the camp compound across from the entrance gate. Males and females ages fifteen and up were obliged to rise at 5:30 in the morning, make their beds, and then attend the head count at the Appellplatz, where they would be counted off before going to their workplaces.

He continued. "Coffee [if you can call the hot black watery liquid that didn't taste anything like coffee by that name] and a slice of bread will be dispensed by the Blockältesten [who usually were Dutch prisoners] early in the mornings; soup or vegetable stew and (if available) sausages around noon, another slice of bread with a bit of cheese, jam, or margarine in the evenings."

This was the menu, delivered in a stolid, impassive voice by the forty-something Blockälteste Josef (Joop) Weiss. As I sat on my bunk listening to him, my heart sank, and I shuddered at the thought of what lay ahead of us. Three slices of bread a day? How long, I thought, would we have to stay in this miserable, godforsaken hole?

"Any food parcels sent by the Red Cross will be distributed to the addressees," Weiss informed us. As far as I can remember, the food parcels never turned up.

"The SS," he went on, "allows us to keep our luggage and clothes, but we are obliged to wear the yellow star on our coats and jackets at all times. This," Weiss pointed out, "is why the SS calls this the Star Camp. Moreover," he concluded his introductory speech, "men and women are permitted to meet throughout the entire day but will live in separate barracks."

And that was it.

The first scary weeks slipped by. The roll calls in particular were wretchedly awful.

At daybreak, Moeder, Vader, and my two brothers went off to work in the Schuhkommando (shoe commando), which was outside in the surrounding area.

It was filthy work that consisted of salvaging usable leather from old shoes or sorting buttons for German army clothing for eleven hours straight. When they returned late in the evening, they all looked dead tired, and I looked at them from across the long table as we ate the thin cabbage soup and saw that Moeder had suddenly aged years. She sat there silent, looking disconsolate and haggard with dark circles under her sunken eyes, just as she had on the first train to Westerbork.

Vader also sat silent, staring dully into his round red metal bowl (which we had been given upon arrival along with a blunt knife, spoon, and fork). As Vader was spooning the watery soup slowly into his mouth, I was reminded of a newsreel scene we had seen many months earlier in Amsterdam (we were still permitted to go to cinemas then) depicting prisoners eating plates of chow in some lockup. The memory made me want to pound my fist on the table and start shouting at the top of my lungs, "Why?" But instead, I bit my lip and kept my mouth shut, staring at Vader as he slowly, stoically lifted the spoon to his lips, lifting it and lowering it, lifting and lowering, lifting, lowering…

What had we done to deserve all this? I still wonder about the evil in the world, why it won't go away. Men are so bestial to each other; they keep fighting and destroying each other. Ah, yes, you will say, why is that? Yes, why? Maybe it's the way human nature works. But is it true? Hard to explain. The fact is human beings are capable of great, wonderful things, make great advances in medicine and science, yet they are the most destructive force that has ever lived on the face of the earth. Why is that? It's a good question. And the further question then arises: Will humans ever change? *Can* they ever change?

TEN

February 1944

Two months had gone by.

The weather in north Germany is cold, very cold, *frigid*, teeth-chattering cold. We huddled in whatever winter clothing we had, but we were constantly chilled to the bone.

The temperature in the winter often hovers below zero, but once the temperature turns milder and snow is falling in silent flakes, it plunges the sloping barracks roofs and heavy forest and watch towers into a white, peaceful silence.

Obligatory roll calls usually would go on for hours.

As the SS started counting us, they would shout abuse and degrading expletives at us and kept counting until we'd be ready to drop.

On a typical morning at ten thirty, the *Arbeitskommandos* (work squads) had already left the camp. Everybody else was ordered outside to attend roll call. "*Appell! Appell!*" (Roll call! Roll call!), the SS hollered in harsh voices, and one of the SS officers standing near the entrance of the camp would join in, blowing the whistle, yelling: "*Raus! Raus! Alle Leute raus. Appell! Appell!*" (Out! Out! Everyone out. Roll call! Roll call!).

All kids below the age of fifteen and the elderly, male and female, hastily lined up outside in the camp square while a group of SS officers huddling in the snow-covered quad conferred in low voices and then

47

started counting, striding briskly up and down the line of inmates, who stood shivering in ranks of five. One of the SS officers, a stocky, thick-chested colonel with thick eyeglasses – probably the group's leader – holding a metal clipboard in his gloved hand started counting the prisoners methodically, pointing with his second finger. He was followed by two groveling staff sergeants, mumbling: "*Hundert zehn*, hundred ten…hundred twenty…thirty…forty…" Then suddenly the group of three men stopped, turned around, and moved toward the group of SS men huddling in their fur-collared winter coats in the middle of the quad.

As all the prisoners stood in the frigid air, the colonel deliberated with the group of SS men, first glancing at his clipboard and then glancing up at his fellow officers. The officer shook his head uncomprehendingly, then turning, walked back toward the inmates and started the roll call again, this time followed by three uniformed subordinates who joined him in the counting.

The colonel counted us slowly and methodically, one by one, while we stood there at attention. We weren't allowed to move or to speak even one word out of the side of our mouths. The snow kept coming from the overcast sky – thick, soft flakes wrapping everything up in a furry-wool stillness as the inmates stood there in silence, shivering in their inadequate overcoats and shoes.

Here and there someone dared to secretly stamp his feet, and then all hell broke loose as the four SS apes started hollering at us, accusing us of being slipshod, not showing up on time for roll call and not properly standing in a row of five, or whatever their excuse was for why the counting as so often had turned out incorrect. But they would quickly calm down and once again go into a huddle and start talking in hushed voices, their breath rising in clouds of steam in the center of the quad.

Then for some reason or other, they would decide to take a break. Good Lord! A break! Often, so often, the SS had counted too many or too few prisoners and now would have to start all over again till they got the numbers right. In the meantime, we had to stand there with chattering teeth in our worn-out clothes without food and drink (or whatever substances they eventually gave us that stood in for food and drink) and wait for the SS men to get back an hour later, after their bellies were comfortably filled, and start counting us again…

Dusk was falling when the wrought-iron camp gate opened. The first *Arbeitskommandos* returned from work, and we still stood there shivering in the numbing cold. Now the *Arbeitskommandos* were forced to join us and stand ramrod-straight at attention until the lucky moment would arrive when the SS finally got their numbers right.

"*Wegtreten! Abtreten! Dismissed!*" Finally the harsh voices of the SS would sweep across the freezing roll call quad, reverberating like a bugler's notes through the air. *W-e-g-t-r-e-t-e-n! Dismissed! Dismissed!*

Almost frozen stiff, we returned to our barracks, nursing our numb feet and hands, and sat on the edge of our beds or at the long wood table trying to warm ourselves with a tin cup of hot "coffee" and a slice of bread and a teaspoon of jam.

The following day, like a broken record, the same routine repeated all over again.

Today, as time goes by, I can clearly recall how an evolution, a barely perceptible development in the prisoners' attitude had taken place. It was the realization that once you stepped inside the camp (read: death camp), it was the same as a death sentence, and you'd better accept the cold reality that one day you would end up dead here. It was a truly unsettling reality to live with.

Admittedly though, tiny glimmers of hope would shimmer through the haze of suffering that if you were lucky, then one day you might come out the other side sane and alive. But the preponderance of prisoners lived with the grim reality that they were condemned to die here. The change in their attitude typically manifested itself in a gradual apathy, a posture of indifference to what was going on around them. The policy was to do whatever the SS orders you to do: stand at attention for hours on end at roll call and keep your mouth shut; go to work and obediently do what the Nazis command you to do; and say to them,

"*Jawohl, Herr Obersturmführer*" (Yes, sir), and say it over and over, and as time passes, listen to your masters' commands like an automaton.

Pretty soon, you may very well think and act like a robot (or slave) and accept your fate, though maybe deep down you still harbor hopes that miracles will happen and one day you will survive this god-awful hellhole. You *obey*, and that's the main thing; you *obey* or else – "We have the means to *make* you obey, prisoner, *understood?*" – and you keep nodding your head silently and sullenly, and you say, "*Jawohl, Herr Unterscharführer,*" or "*Bitte schön, Herr Obersturmführer,*" and you bow your head obsequiously and you say, "*Danke schön, Herr Standartenführer,*" yes, please, thank you, sir, like a broken record, always with the repeating refrain of the German politeness.

Looking back on it now, it seems to me that the life we spent in the camp seemed analogous to the fate of a soldier in war; once he is baptized by fire and has acknowledged and *accepted* his fate of dying, he won't turn and flee. No, setting his jaw firm and gritting his teeth, he will keep on fighting doggedly, not giving in, driving hard. That was the same philosophy many of us lived by in the camp, doggedly and obstinately hell bent on survival, not giving in, come hell or high water, thinking we were going to make it until liberty came…maybe this week…maybe next week…maybe a month…but we were going to make it. I recall how I often stood there and wondered, *How long, how many days? And what will the future bring?* But the thought of death never entered my mind. What I wanted was to get out of this filthy hole and be where there was food, enough glorious food.

ELEVEN

~

Bergen-Belsen – July 1944

As the weeks and then months passed, a visible change in the prisoners' demeanor became quite noticeable. There was a gruff irascibility, a kind of aggressive meanness, not giving a fig about your fellow prisoners one way or the other. You only kept looking out for yourself, made damn sure to save your own skin, tried your best to survive, and to hell with everything else – that's right, to hell with everybody and everything else – which was a pretty awful way to live our lives.

On the other hand, there were other inmates, regrettably more often than not, who went through this phase and in the end simply turned phlegmatic, lived in that unconscious state of agonized numbness and wouldn't care about anything anymore. They'd sit and stare into empty space with an apathetic, haggard look on their skin-and-bones faces, give a resigned shrug and think, *whatever*. Yeah, whatever. Come what may, they couldn't care less…and would fade away, ending up in cardiovascular collapse and quick death.

There's one incident that's indelibly etched on my memory.

One morning – it must have been around late July – a transport of a few hundred French people arrived from the Drancy transit camp, outside Paris. They were mostly young men and women. One of them, a tall, dark-haired, slim Frenchman, about nineteen years old, who had been assigned to our barracks was sitting across from me at the empty table. He ate his bread ration, *the entire portion* he received upon arrival (the slice of bread with a scoop of white cheese on top) in several huge bites as if he were sitting back home at the kitchen table having a quiet breakfast snack. We other prisoners sat there staring at him with disbelieving eyes. Apparently, the man had no idea what lay ahead of him.

A few months later, we were sitting one evening at the same table spooning our watery cabbage soup when a hollow-cheeked Dutchman in his fifties – he was all skin and bones – suddenly got up from the table, dashed as fast as his legs could carry him across the floor, grasped a large slice of bread that was lying unheeded on someone's bottom bunk, and was about to run off with it when one of the prisoners sitting near me shouted at him, "Hey, you! Come back here!"

Now, caught in the act of stealing, the man stopped dead in his tracks. The slice of bread he had grabbed belonged to the Frenchman who upon his arrival had devoured his entire ration (the entire ration!) in a few huge bites like a kid gobbling up sweets in a candy store.

The Frenchman, Michel, innocent and green as he was, never had thought that anybody would steal bread from him, and so he hadn't bothered hiding the bread from view.

We sat there and watched in stunned disbelief as that bony, skeletal Dutchman stood there momentarily hesitating, mulling over his options. He could give it back and shut up, or he could try to talk the Frenchman into letting him have a piece, which was improbable.

Seeing no other way, the Dutchman suddenly broke a large piece off the bread, quickly stuffed it into his mouth, hastily chewed, then broke off another piece, a larger one, and jubilantly wolfed it down. Now, Michel the Frenchman jumped to his feet and together with another inmate tackled him (though it must be said, a little puff from someone's lips and the Dutchman would have drifted away like a feather) and punched him in the jaw. The Dutchman fell to the floor, gasping for air, then shrieking and kicking away at the two of them, trying to hold on to his beloved little piece of bread. The Frenchman's comrade wrenched it away from him and handed it over to Michel, who, cursing viciously, started kicking the Dutch guy in the head. The Dutchman lay there writhing and moaning and crying in a weepy voice, "D-don't hurt me, please."

Most of us just sat there looking on in sullen silence. Picturing this pathetic scene, seeing this skeleton lying there in the barracks room begging for a little piece of bread while being kicked and mauled, gives you an inkling of what people were facing in such situations when they were fighting for their very survival. In such a moment, the evil, the beast in men will get unmasked and be uncovered like a microbe under the microscope.

As the days dragged into weeks and then months, the face of the camp changed. The SS had been rarely seen. Here and there they could be seen walking singly or in pairs or riding on motorcycles with side-cars on the camp's main road.

Now the black-bereted *Kapos* wearing white arm bands (with the bold black lettering "KAPO") had made their appearance. These over-seers generally were a bunch of former convicts, all sorts of vicious criminals.

The inmates' days usually were spent at work, at a place not far from outside of the camp. As dawn broke, *Kapos* would barge in yell-ing, "Get up. Wake up. *Los, los*. Fast, *schnell!*" and the prisoners would get up, get dressed, gulp down the cup of "coffee," swallow the piece of bread, and then would be marched off to several places, always accom-panied by two or three *Kapos* or armed SS guards. Then by sundown, looking tired, humiliated, beat, miserable, and irritated, they would be back inside the camp. By then the gates of the camp would get locked by the SS from the outside.

This was the way prisoners spent their days. Most inmates kept to themselves. That was true of my two brothers – they'd get up in the morning, would get marched off, and many hours later got back from their work shifts. Actually, we didn't see much of each other.

I hardly can remember the time we spent together outside of seeing each other when sitting and eating on the bunk beds or at the table next to other cheerless inmates who hardly would talk except of their tedious, endless hours' work. And then the next morning like a broken record, the new day started again; getting up, gulping the "coffee," swallowing the slice of bread, and then already being aware of what was lying ahead, they would go apathetically off to work – and that was it.

And that kept us going and breathing and hoping.

We youngsters – aged between twelve and fourteen – stayed back in the barracks. There were four of us, and we were friends. One was blond Kees Graaf, the other was Henk de Vries, and then there was small, curly-haired thirteen-year-old Uriel de Jong, who hailed from Rotterdam. We spent a lot of time together, talked wistfully about the days when we would be free again, thinking nostalgically of the free world we'd once known.

We would be sitting in chairs in the sun in front of the barracks and would fantasize about delicious mouthwatering hamburger sandwiches dripping with grease or delicious sunny-side up eggs and juicy steaks with fluffy mashed potatoes served up on silver trays, and we would say to each other, "Hey, take your pick," and one of us, usually Henk, would smack his lips with a long slurping sound, miming that he was munching on something delicious…and as I sat listening to their reminiscing, I suddenly found myself thinking if only I had wings and could fly, fly like an eagle so high, soar through the deep blue sky, away from this godforsaken hellhole. If I could just glide like a stately ship to the free world and *be free* like a bird, oh, how wonderful that would be. But then my thoughts would switch back to where we were now, and I asked myself *what will the next couple of months bring*, and then the thought of freedom faded away.

And then again, as lots of rumors swirled around the camp about an Allied invasion, we were thinking maybe in a few weeks, maybe in a month, maybe even sooner – perhaps as early as next week – yes, who knew?

TWELVE

The Air Raid

One morning, after roll call and after the *Arbeitskommandos* had left, I stepped out of the barracks and headed in the still early morning toward the outdoor latrine at the edge of a pine forest.

As I stepped inside, I glanced around.

The place was deserted. Well, I told myself, you're better off being here than in the barracks where the toilet cubicles are constantly out of order.

One minute went by, and I heard the piercing sound of a wailing air raid siren outside. Then silence. I frowned. What was that all about?

A distant humming was growing closer and closer, and then *boom*! A deafening roar passed over the latrine that made the floor under me shudder as though an earthquake was about to split the earth apart.

Seconds later came the second thundering sound of an aircraft flying over.

I rushed outside and glanced up. Two planes circled overhead. They swooped out of the deep blue sky with an ear-splitting roar, and then the rattling of machine guns began.

Then another flame-spitting plane roared past. *Woosh!* And *boom* it went. And another. It was twinkling in the sunlight. Staring at them, I was filled with sudden euphoria. *The camp is under attack!* I thought. *Maybe the rumors have been true after all. Maybe the Allies have come to free us.* I didn't dare consider that our misery was about to come to an end. I was young, but the past few years had beaten the naivete out of me.

One hundred yards from me, a small group of youngsters had appeared outside the barracks. They were shielding their eyes with their hands from the sun, staring excitedly into the sky.

They were calling out something and then suddenly scattered like pins in a bowling alley when another fighter plane with the British blue and red circles clearly visible on its wings leapt over the forest tree tops, firing at full blast at the lookout towers. It missed the target. Then another plane thundered across, this time spraying the left tower with canon fire, blowing it up into a huge fireball.

As I was standing rooted to the spot, I watched a line of bullets furiously stitching across the concrete, kicking up small stones and dirt. It occurred to me in a flash of insight that I might be knocked down by the sudden canon burst. Frightened, I ran behind the latrine for cover and hit the dirt. I lay there huddled as close to the ground as I could as the low-flying strafing planes flew over several times. And then as suddenly as they had come, the planes were gone, and an eerie silence had settled over the camp.

It had been a matter of maybe two minutes, and then the attack was over.

I got up and saw command vehicles pulling up and SS men leaping out on the asphalt road beyond the barbed wire, cursing and hollering at the prisoners to get the hell back into the barracks or into the trenches we had been forced to dig a few weeks earlier.

We saw a column of black smoke rising slowly into the sky behind the pine forest and later learned that the planes had bombed and destroyed an ammunition depot and a fire range. Later, back in our barracks, there was much discussion of the prisoners' disappointment that the planes hadn't bothered to bomb the SS barracks. Why had they spared the Nazi barracks? I heard one man say he felt like a bride waiting with excitement at her wedding ceremony only to have her groom not show.

Clearly the world had forgotten us, and we had no choice but to wait – wait till the Allies would break through German defense line and liberate us. Or wait until the Germans were beaten down into submission and defeat, because it was obvious they were losing the war. Even the lowest of the low – the Jews and Roma and others who joined me in this camp – even we knew the Germans were losing the war. But how long would it take for the country to abandon Hitler?

And how many of us would still be alive?

A few weeks later, during the month of September 1944, we heard about the Allied landing in Normandy on the west coast of France, and rumors were buzzing that the Allies had already invaded the first villages in southern France and now pushed deeper and deeper into the country. When we went to bed at night, we could hear the humming, droning sound of Allied fighter planes flying overhead above the clouds on their way to Germany to drop tons of bombs on the German cities. Picturing it – actually *seeing* in my mind the pilots opening the bay doors of the planes, releasing their loads of bombs upon the hated German towns – filled me with immense satisfaction. One glimmer of hope kept blinking at us like a flickering neon tube: *Could the rumors be true? Were the Allies winning the war against the Nazis? Could our freedom be close at hand?*

And that kept us going and breathing and hoping.

THIRTEEN

Thirteen at Midnight

Summer and autumn had passed, and we faced another cold winter in Bergen-Belsen.

On Tuesday evening, December 27, 1944, a cold week, Vader had set aside his daily bread ration and had asked some acquaintances to come to our barracks for a minyan and a brief celebration of my bar mitzvah. Around midnight, ten men quietly gathered in silence between the three-tiered bunk beds as I softly recited the blessing my father had taught me earlier, which men recite when called to the Torah.

"*Barchu es Hashem hamevorach.*"

And the men responded, "*Baruch Hashem hamevorach l'olam va'ed.*"

I continued, "*Baruch Attah Hashem Elokeinu Melech ha'olam asher bachar banu mi'kol ha'amim v'nasan lanu es Toraso. Baruch Attah Hashem, nosein haTorah.*"

Then Vader said the special blessing of *baruch shepetarani* said by the father of a boy who has reached the age of bar mitzvah. There was a hearty mazel tov. Father proudly slapped me on my shoulder and then he gave everyone a piece of the ration he had saved up for a bar mitzvah "meal." Afterwards, everybody returned to their bunks and went back to sleep.

It had been a pretty tense moment doing this ritual, hidden between the silent rows of three-tiered bunk beds, making sure that no one would see us. All religious practice was forbidden by the Nazis and harshly punished. I don't know if they had any religion other than that of conquering and killing.

The next evening when my parents came back from work, a great surprise awaited me. Gray-haired Josef Weiss, the head of the barracks, presented me with a big smile and my bar mitzvah present: *a delicious fresh loaf of bread!*

Staring at it, my eyes nearly popped out of my head. My mouth started watering just thinking of eating a crusty piece of that bread. I'm not kidding, holding the loaf in my hand, I felt like the owner of a 24-karat gold bar. This present was irreplaceable. I would not have traded it for anything in the world. For nothing. Period.

Anyone who hasn't been in captivity in a Nazi camp suffering from this awful gnawing hunger can't imagine what it was like to receive such a present. A whole loaf of bread! Can you believe it? *A loaf of fresh bread!* Oh, boy. I did not spend time wondering how Weiss had managed to obtain it, though as I write this, I try to unravel whom he would have had to bribe – and with what – to find me this priceless gift.

For just an instant, I was overcome by the urge to wolf down the entire loaf right then and there. I looked at a knife that was lying on the table nearby and imagined quickly cutting a big chunk off the bread and swallowing it.

A glorious moment!

Moeder and Vader, who had been present when Meneer (Mr.) Weiss had handed me the bread, cautiously told me that we'd better ration it carefully over the next couple of days (recently, food rations had become increasingly meager), and as Moeder, smiling gently, took hold of the bread, in my mind's eye I saw a thief climbing into my room trying to take the bicycle I had received for my seventh birthday. I bit back what I wanted to say – "Hey, that's my present!" – and wisely kept my mouth shut. What the heck was I thinking, anyway? Would I have been so heartless as to eat the bread up all by myself while my parents and brothers sat there watching me gobble it up without giving them a single crumb? Now I waited and watched with a sinking heart as Moeder, biting her lower lip in concentration, started arranging for little portions, making notch marks with the knife along the top edge of the loaf of bread.

We needed a secure hideout for it. In our old life, we would put possessions in a safe place, maybe in a safe deposit box, but here we had only the recess of a bunk to keep things hidden from prying eyes.

In the end, I was happy I was able to share my gift with my family. After all, what could be more of a gift to myself than helping to keep alive the people who meant most to me? And this was not to be taken for granted, as we would all see just one short week later.

Daybreak. The gates had been closed after the labor detail in ranks of five left the camp. That morning after roll call, I made my way to the barracks where my friends lived. I found them sitting on a bench near the door, looking concerned.

I asked them, "Is there any problem?"

Kees sat staring at me.

"It's about your mother."

"My mother?"

"Yes."

I felt my stomach plummet.

"What about her?"

Kees filled me in on what had happened while Uriel sat there silently, not giving any comment.

Apparently, Moeder had arrived late at the assembly place that morning and had missed her labor detail as they marched off to work in the pre-dawn darkness.

"Now the SS are going to make her stand all night long at the elec-trified barbed-wire fence," Kees told me.

"What?" I said, disbelieving.

I was shocked and didn't know what to say. Standing in front of the gate in the icy wind all night till daybreak while guards were patrolling in front of you was a nightmare. Quite a few prisoners who had been punished this way had simply gone over the edge, flinging themselves on the fence as they tried to climb over it and were electrocuted.

In fact, I had watched one morning as prisoners pulled a corpse across the stony square toward the crematoria. I couldn't bear to think about Moeder being –

No.

When the darkness thickened, I went to see Moeder at her barracks. She stood in the corner of the room listening as Weiss was speaking to her. I moved toward them. Weiss talked insistently to her.

"They want you to feel intimidated," he told her. "There's no reason to be afraid of anything. You'll be fine. Here."

He handed her a pile of old German newspapers he had found in the back of one of the buildings.

I stared at the papers. I vaguely recall reading the headlines. "*Immer mehr Bomben*" (More and more bombs), "*Deutschland im Kriegszustand*" (Germany in state of war), "*Der Landsturm*" (The reserve forces)…

"Put on several layers of clothing," Weiss advised her. "Here. Put the newspapers between your clothes and wrap your entire body and feet in them to keep warm."

She thanked Weiss, and he turned and went out the door back into the gathering darkness.

I sat down, and we talked for ten minutes. I looked across at her and saw the tension in her face. Vader and my brothers had also come to see her, and she told me that everything would be fine.

Before I left, she looked me in the eye and said calmly, "Hey, don't worry, Wolfi. I'll be all right."

I nodded. Filled with dread, I turned away.

The next morning, after I left the men's barracks where I slept and stepped into her barracks, I found Moeder lying under the blanket on her bunk.

I took a seat across from her, and she explained what had happened.

Among the SS who had been on duty during the night was a guard named Pavlenko, who had kept watching Moeder like a hawk, taunting her and prodding her with the tip of his rifle, while making sneering remarks.

She told me that as she fought sleep all night, she would take deep breaths and try to control her emotions. As she stood shivering in the icy cold, she would think about us having a wonderful new life in peace, owning our own little home and never returning to Germany. In her mind, she could see the Swiss Alps in summer where she grew up as a child. She immersed herself in seeing the peaceful scenery and imagining hearing the soothing sound of distant cow bells...

The last one or two hours, she had been shivering uncontrollably and was almost too weak to move or stand. All she needed, she said, was a little crumb of bread or something to drink. When the first light of dawn light had appeared, a prisoner-foreman had escorted her back to the barracks, where, physically and emotionally exhausted, she had fallen into bed and instantly gone to sleep.

When prisoners standing at the fence for about eight hours straight as a punishment became weak or began to shake or almost fainted and dropped to the ground, nothing delighted the SS and *Kapos* more than to kick their faces and club them senseless with a baton or with the butts of their carbines. It was a game they enjoyed playing.

FOURTEEN

No Exit

At the end of January 1945, the day we had longed for came. An exchange with German prisoners of war was imminent. Those South American passports that set us apart were finally going to be useful.

On January 20, 1945, the commandant's office informed us that inmates holding South or Central American passports should pack their bags and get ready to report to the camp gate at ten o'clock the following morning. All told, 301 prisoners were selected to go to Switzerland. Switzerland! Can you believe it?

Filled with joy, my parents, my brothers, and I hugged one another. We sat up a long time talking excitedly (as though we were already in Switzerland) about what we were going to do and where we would go.

Somewhat later, we set about packing our stuff.

All through that Sunday night till daybreak, there were not many of us who slept. Our minds were racing. Had the horror and dread of the past years finally come to an end? Was this really the end of our misery?

We found it hard to believe. But it was the truth. It was not like when you wake up from a bad dream and you think, *thank goodness it was just a dream.* No, *this* was *real.* This was liberation. This was freedom. What words. *Freedom. Liberty.* Very soon, we would stop seeing the hated SS guards and the *Kapos* and the camp gates. We would be different people.

As we lucky ones started packing our stuff, the less fortunate people turned to look at us with barely concealed envy on their faces. Seeing us – the jubilant ones – already living a life of freedom, without fear and terror, they looked as though the last ray of hope suddenly had vanished right before their eyes.

Early the following morning, before any *Arbeitskommandos* left, relatives and friends came over, shook hands with us, smiled, and wished us all the best with that wistful expression on their faces that said, "Oh, you lucky ones," and we patted their backs and told them to keep their chins up – next time, they might be on the list and be out of here, so cheer up. But it was a depressing moment as we shook hands and said goodbye to them.

That Sunday, at ten a.m., we stood with packed bags and huddled beneath a chilly gray sky as an SS woman and SS guard emerged from a black Volkswagen car in front of the gate and entered the camp.

Helga Krumm, a short, sturdy SS Aufseherin (female overseer) in khaki jacket and green SS cap, was holding a list of names in hand.

SS guard Lukas Pavlenko, stony-faced, his arms folded across his broad chest, stood there in a wide-legged position watching everything attentively. He was the Nazi guard who saw to it that everything would go like clockwork, without a hitch. At roll calls, he would sometimes stand at the gate, his cold eyes paying close attention to the inmate count, waiting for someone to step out of line so he could punish them with a fierce beating.

SS Aufseherin Krumm stood studying our group for a moment before addressing us in German. "I'll call up all persons who were selected for this exchange transport. Anyone absent because of illness cannot – I repeat, cannot – go, and will stay here." She added, "You have to be fit for the prisoner exchange." This was significant; since the mass influx of deported Jews from the east, many prisoners had fallen ill with pneumonia, tuberculosis, and uncontrollable diarrhea.

She paused a moment. "When I call your names, I want everybody to raise his hand and identify himself."

Well, I thought to myself, *Moeder, Vader, my brothers, and I are fine.* There was no problem here, so we waited.

The SS overseer glanced stonily about at the stoic faces of the prisoners who surrounded her. She raised the clipboard and began to call the first names, her sharp voice sounding uncannily hollow in the cold, damp air: "Isi Cohen…"

A hand went up. "Here."

Helga Krumm nodded at Pavlenko, who motioned the inmate to the first truck in the convoy that had pulled up while we were standing there, waiting to take the prisoners to the train.

"Reuven de Vries…"

Another hand went up.

"Samuel Horwitz…and Sarah Horowitz."

Two hands went up. Sarah Horowitz turned to SS guard Pavlenko, who pointed to the waiting truck.

Krumm studied the clipboard a moment.

"Philip Wagenaar…"

"Yes."

A beat of silence.

Krumm took out a pen and wrote something down.

"Benjamin and Rachel Klaassen."

"*Jawohl.*"

The first truck began to fill up.

This went on for ten minutes. We waited impatiently for our names to be called. Relatives who stood beside us were called up. They raised their hands, smiled at us, and happily boarded the truck.

We looked after them, shivering in the cold, and wondered how long we would have to wait for our names to be called.

I watched a flock of white birds circling overhead. They were flapping their wings, wheeling and swooping, then soared in the air and flew away into freedom…

Longingly, I stared after them.

The minutes crawled on.

We stood waiting in the shivery weather wondering how much longer. Then SS Aufseherin Krumm's voice called out our names: "Regina Rachel Holles." Then: "Ephraim Victor, Joseph, and Wolf Holles," and Moeder, my father and brother, and I raised our hands and responded, "Yes."

And then she called out, "Elias Holles," my oldest brother (he was seventeen years old then), and he put his hand up and said, "Here."

At that moment, a visibly upset stocky woman, holding a small girl's hand, hurried forward, pushed her way through the waiting crowd, stopped in front of the startled-looking SS warden, and got entangled in a loud argument with her.

Before we were able to proceed, we had to wait for an affirmative nod from SS Aufseherin Krumm. And so we waited.

What we were able to make out from their rapidly spoken German was that Aufseherin Krumm had omitted reading the child's name off the list, even after the mother had pointed a finger at the scared little thing now standing beside her with lowered eyes.

The mother kept talking in a stream. She pointed to her daughter. "*Hier ist sie!*" she cried out. "She is here!"

Aufseherin Krumm raised a hand to stop her, consulted the clipboard for a moment, and after some more back-and-forth discussion with the woman, the warden reluctantly gave in and let them board the truck. Why the warden was reluctant to acknowledge the right of the woman and daughter to leave this horrible hell was a mystery. There would be another prisoner to take her place, no doubt.

After that, Helga Krumm paused a moment, studied the clipboard again, glanced up at the group, and said, curtly, "Elias Holles didn't answer my call. *Na schön*," she shrugged, "too bad, apparently the young man is sick," and with a crisp flick of her wrist, she drew a line through his name. Then glancing up again, she said uncaringly, "The family is crossed off the list."

It took a moment for Aufseherin Krumm's words to sink in. *Had the woman just removed us from the transport to freedom?*

It couldn't be true. Impossible. We could not believe our ears.

"*Nein, nein,* no, no," Moeder exclaimed, pointing a finger frantically, "*das ist falsch!* You are wrong, my son is here, he's not sick, look, here, he's right here!"

The whole group turned toward us.

"*Where* is he?" Krumm looked down at her in cold contempt. "Where's your son?"

"He's right here!" Moeder exclaimed, pointing a finger to my brother and then turning back to her. "He's *here!*"

The SS woman turned to look at Elie, who stood there, shocked, quickly raising his arm and nodding his head.

"*Nein, nein,* no, no," the Nazi overseer persisted firmly, shaking her head stubbornly. "I told you," she snapped. "I know what I am doing." She paused. "You go back to your barracks. All of you. Right now. Move it! *Vorwärts!*" Her eyes bored stonily into my mother's. Aufseherin Krumm paused again then, ignoring Moeder, and watched impassively as the shivering group of prisoners huddled together like soon-to-be-butchered lambs.

We looked at each other, dazed, not yet fully comprehending what was happening. Wringing her hands, Moeder kept imploring the Nazi warden. "You don't understand, please, please, please, I beg you, my son is all right, he is not sick. He's strong and healthy. He's *right here!*" she cried despairingly, pointing her finger to him.

"*Ach, so?* Oh, yes?" Unmoved, hands on hips, eyebrows raised, Aufseherin Krumm swung around toward the SS guard, giving him a slight nod of the head, and the young guard quickly strode over to Moeder and ordered her to move.

"Move it!" he snapped. "Move it!"

Moeder stood there still like a stubborn mule.

Enraged now, the guard barked, "Go!"

Moeder, as though deaf, refused to budge.

"Get moving, damn it!"

Moeder stared at him, not moving.

"I told you," the guard roared, "Move!"

Moeder muttered under her breath, "It's not fair! It's not fair!" She shook her head from side to side. "It's not fair! No, I can't believe it!"

She turned to the SS woman, raised her hands imploringly, and begged her to please, please, please let her family board the truck.

Prisoners standing near us, looking scared, turned their heads away.

The SS warden looked across at the guard named Pavlenko and waved her hand at him. It was a signal.

The Nazi guard nodded. He stepped forward, stared at Moeder, quietly removed a hardwood truncheon from his pocket, and as a sort of a warm-up switched the club from his left hand to his right, then, emotionless, struck a dozen vicious blows on Moeder's head and shoulders. Moeder held up her hands protectively, trying to escape the blows raining down on her. I stood rooted to the spot, feeling helpless. *I've got to stop this vile Nazi striking her*, I thought, and suddenly envisioned myself being Popeye the Sailor Man. In my imagination, I saw myself grabbing this big-boned brute by the collar, lifting him up, and fearlessly ordering him to let her go. But in reality, I did nothing. I just stood trembling with terror, my legs shaking fearfully, unable to lift a finger.

Vader was shocked too, but he rushed at that Nazi guard to stop his insane beatings. Pavlenko, startled, let go, and now turned toward Vader, his eyes flat and inexpressive, one hand furiously pulling to get his pistol from his black holster flap and jam it into Vader's face.

Vader had stopped dead in his tracks and stood there motionless like a still frame from a film. From that point on, maybe because of the shock I felt, everything seemed to slow down. Vader was slowly putting his arm around Moeder's shoulder and she, looking distraught, was slowly pushing a strand of hair out of her fear-ridden eyes. As we headed back to the barracks, that exemplary member of the SS guard, slipping the truncheon back into his pocket, stood there imperially with both arms folded across his chest like a king before his bowing subjects, smiling amiably at the departing group of prisoners as though nothing out of the ordinary had happened.

In hindsight, I can say, with one hundred percent certainty, that this episode changed our lives forever. It was as if the jury had cleared the defendant, but the judge sent him back to prison.

How were we going to face the daily gloomy routine, the freezing roll calls, the filth and dirt and starvation? How were we to keep going?

Was the guard Pavlenko complicit in the wrongdoing?

Had Krumm been the catalyst?

You bet.

It would have been an easy thing for them to recheck things, and everything would have been just fine. But no, these two didn't even want to know the truth. It was like throwing a tiny pebble into a pond and watching the ripples spread. Just a little itty-bitty pebble made unforeseen things open up. Little ripples, big waves. And so it was.

By some bad stroke of luck, this Nazi overseer with outstretched arm, pointing a finger at us, ordering us to remain, to shut up and stay put, had changed everything. Call it fate or tough luck, call it Divine Providence. You may call it anything you want. It didn't matter anymore, it didn't matter anymore.

And from this moment on, things started to go downhill.

FIFTEEN

Quirk of Fate

The war went on. By January 1945, the conditions in the camp had worsened; the number of prisoners greatly increased, and our camp was expanded to accommodate Jews who had been evacuated from camps in the east. Barracks that usually would house about 120 prisoners now were filled to overflowing, with people lying on the floor and tents set up outside. Water and food supplies continued to shrink. The head of the barracks, it turned out, had been informed by the SS that truckloads of food moving across the autobahn had been the target of air strikes. (Later we would learn that this was a false report.)

I remember I felt pretty sick.

I had been suffering from a persistent dysentery that had become almost chronic. It was the food – if you can call this murky brown-colored liquid and the few slices of stale bread food – that must have caused it. Whatever I ate, which had been dismally little (unfortunately, the bar mitzvah bread was long gone), poured out of me like water, and I headed for the outdoor latrine almost 24/7. I recall staring down at my body in horror, seeing the ribs and chest bones protruding through an almost yellowish transparent skin.

The image that stays imprinted on my mind was that cold morning as I sat with my buddy Kees Graaf outside in the wintry sun and we talked about what we were going to do once we got back home after the war.

I had noticed that he looked different. He was thin as a rail and his face had turned white – almost gray. Suddenly he fell silent, just sitting there in his chair, his eyes closed as though he had fallen asleep.

I leaned forward. "Hey, Kees!"

Silence.

I looked at him. "You okay, Kees?"

He sat there, silent, not responding. I sat forward and shook him by the shoulder.

"Hey, Kees, wake up!"

I stared at him. His head fell sideways. He didn't move. His mouth was slightly open. I realized then that he was dead. I went for help. Shortly afterwards, two men of the special unit arrived, lifted him onto a gurney, and carried him away.

He had died as he sat there in a chair across from me and we talked about Dutch soccer players and the Champions League.

That was Kees, my buddy who once, not so long ago, had day-dreams of food, imagined eating strawberries with whipped cream and delicious pastrami sandwiches, smacking his lips with relish, and now he had ceased to exist. Fourteen years old. Now he was gone. Like dust in the wind. I wanted to cry for him, but I couldn't. I had gotten too hardened to grieve for anyone.

A few hours later, I stood watching an open trailer loaded with piles of corpses passing by. The truck was on its way to the crematorium. As it passed, I spotted a bony arm dangling from the heap and suddenly thought to myself maybe it belonged to Kees – maybe that was his arm up there among the pile of corpses. I stood there staring after the truck as it headed for the gate and watched until it was out of sight up the road. *Goodbye*, I thought, *goodbye, buddy, rest in peace.*

Days went by. The SS was seen less and less, and in their stead the hard-looking *Kapos* became more visible. A brutal reign of terror descended upon us; swinging their hardwood truncheons with sadistic pleasure, these *Kapos* would beat up prisoners at random. They would order us to stand as straight as a pole during the roll calls, and at daybreak they'd wake us by rattling their truncheons against the metal bunks' bedposts, their voices snarling brutally: "Off your beds, you lazy swine! No Sabbath today. Hurry up! Hurry up!" And the rattling sound of their wooden clubs along the bedposts, instilling cold terror into us, seemed to go on and on incessantly.

Seated in my apartment today, I am still flooded by memories of the camp. Fear and terror gripped us. We were deathly afraid of the *Kapos* and the vicious SS. Just observing their demeanor and crass truculent arrogance toward us was enough to strike terror into brave hearts. We feared that at any given moment, one of those monsters would calmly remove a gun from his holster, take aim at one of us and then squeeze the trigger and shoot us in the head in cold blood. This would not be in the least surprising.

Anyone who has been incarcerated in a Nazi death camp or under some other ruthless dictatorship knows. He knows of the evil slumbering in human beings. Hand a whip to this or that person and tell him he is in command of another person and see, just watch how this man will change in a short period of time. He will turn into a cruel, vicious brute; he will feel superior and will wield his power ruthlessly. No, surely not everybody will act this way, but this definitely was the case with these Nazi officers, who often had joined the ranks voluntarily. An SS officer would commit the most barbaric crimes and then go back home to his family and behave like an ordinary human being, like a father or husband, love his devoted wife and at night tuck his little children into bed and sing sentimental lullabies to them.

The final phase till liberation was a total blur, a disjointed sequence of pictures, a kind of thought memory consisting of impressions of mortally sick prisoners, eyes sunk deep in their heads, their bones sticking out like flag poles from their bodies, absolute skeletons, looking inhuman with smudged, yellowed faces, their unseeing eyes gazing, mouths hanging open in a near-final death agony, seeming to ask, when is it finally going to end?

Rumor had it that the Allied forces were now nearing the German heartland. The motto was: Do. Not. Give. Up. Hang in there. Freedom is near…

It was, but not for everyone.

Uriel de Jong, my friend from Rotterdam who used to hang out with me, had died. He hadn't been seen for a few days, and it didn't take us long to find out why.

As Henk (my remaining friend) and I entered his barracks, we saw two men from the burial detail who had come to fetch him. They found him lying curled up on his side on the top bunk. Apparently, rigor mortis had already set in. They seized him by wrists and ankles, and as we stood there watching, lifted his body off the bunk bed onto a makeshift stretcher, muttering disgustedly under their breaths that no one had been looking after him as he was lying there, dying like a dog. They tried to straighten him from his curled-up position and then carried him off to a truck waiting outside. If memory serves me correctly, he lasted about thirteen months after his arrival in the camp. Watching my buddies die had become a daily habit. You got used to it. Like tying your shoelaces or wearing your everyday shirt.

I often found myself listening to prisoners sitting on the edge of their beds in the barracks debating the unpredictable whims of fate, discussing why Ruben so-and-so and not Simon so-and-so had died. Why did this woman die and not the other? Why he? Why not she? Why?

In retrospect, it seems to me that in a war, when bullets and shells are flying about, and your friend Chuck or Billy or Gary standing near you cries out, "I got hit!" and suddenly crumples like a floppy rag doll to the ground dead, and you keep going, hoping to survive this hell and stay safe, if you had a moment to think, you might be filled with wonder at the baffling unpredictability of death. Why does one person live through this hell and others don't? Quirk of fate? Maybe you were the lucky one and drew the winning ticket, but others didn't get that far. You tell me.

And the prisoners kept debating and hoping…

There were people who were religiously observant and held on to their faith, deeply convinced that God would look after them, but others would shrug it off unimpressed and say, after all this anguish and death and horror, how can you still harbor any beliefs? Certainly, I learned there were instances when nonbelievers after they had survived the camps became observant, while others lost their faith. All of us tried to hold on like a drowning man clinging to a life preserver, in whatever way we could at the time.

SIXTEEN

Toward the End of It

From the wretched day that we were thrown off the transport, Vader had given up hope he'd ever make it out alive. He looked discouraged and emaciated, and he kept to himself, hardly talking to us.

When coming back from work (he was now assigned to the kitchen detail), he lay down on his bunk, crossed his arms behind his head, and brooded. Moeder came to the barracks and sat there quietly by his bedside. She too did not talk much.

What was the point? Nothing was going to change. We had to persevere and hope the war would be over soon. The words so often spoken, "*Hang in there*," mocked us as we tried to come to grips with the new situation.

Around us the chaos deepened. Food supplies continued to dwindle. People around us dropped like flies of diseases and starvation, in very large numbers. The lack of sanitary conditions was horrendous. Lice attacked us like a pack of wild dogs.

The SS got noticeably nervous. They moved about irritably and impatiently held roll calls, notwithstanding the freezing sleet and icy downpours drenching us to the skin. But sometimes – was it out of mercy or were they just looking after themselves? – they shortened the hours-long roll calls.

We had noticed a Dutchman named Bernard De Witt behaving in a strangely irrational manner. This tall and now totally emaciated man was still handsome, in his early twenties with unruly sandy hair and a good-natured, friendly smile. He, like us, had been crossed off the exchange list, and he had changed after that. We learned later that SS guard Pavlenko had observed De Witt having coughing bouts with excessive phlegm and judged him unfit for the prisoner exchange.

I remember when the six of us – my family and De Witt – had been taken off the exchange list and had returned to our barracks, De Witt, deeply depressed, kept muttering to himself, "I can't take this anymore. Enough is enough." He said it over and over. "It can't go on like this. Something's got to give. Something's got to give." Shaking his head despondently, like a madman he kept repeating it to himself over and over.

One day, seated at the long table in the barracks, drinking the dirty brownish water, he was coughing from time to time but controlled it. All of a sudden, his eyes glittering madly, he lifted up his cup and poured the hot coffee with a contemptuous sneer onto the table. Then he jumped up from his chair, pranced around, cursed and yelled, then climbed onto the low table and started dancing, laughing maniacally and talking gibberish.

We sat watching him and at first thought it uproariously funny, but soon, it wasn't funny anymore.

Another time, having saved his quarter loaf of bread, De Witt started scattering crumbs around like confetti and watched with roaring laughter as the men dived for the crumbs and then again started frolicking on the table. A group of prisoners managed to calm him down and put him to bed, and he fell asleep peacefully on his bunk. When he awoke the next morning, De Witt was his mild self again and acted normally.

This odd ritual or quirk of De Witt's happened every few days.

Josef Weiss, the head of the barracks, had reported him sick to the SS staff, and for a couple of days De Witt didn't attend roll call.

Then things took a turn for the worse. One morning the SS started the count and found one prisoner missing. When they consulted with

Blockälteste Weiss and found out prisoner De Witt hadn't shown up for the morning roll call, they hit the roof.

"*What?!*" SS Obersturmführer Weber, a long-necked, narrow-chested man, roared at Weiss furiously. The officer's thick-lensed eyeglasses were soaking wet from the morning sleet. "He's *refusing* to fall in for roll call?" He took a deep breath, adjusted his steel-rimmed glasses with thumb and forefinger, then half bent over at the waist, his nose almost touching the Blockälteste's startled face, repeated, unbelieving, "*Was? Er weigert sich auf dem Appellplatz anzutreten?*" (What?! He *refuses* to fall in for roll call?). He stared at Weiss from under his thick brows as though Weiss had gone mad.

Weiss, wisely enough, said nothing.

"And may I ask," the SS officer asked in a sardonic tone, "why he refuses to report for roll call?"

Weiss kept quiet.

"*Antworten Sie!*" (Answer me!), Weber barked, his breath clouding the freezing air.

"The prisoner," Weiss replied timidly, "has reported sick. He's unable to stand on his feet for a long time."

"*Ach, so*, I see," the Sturmführer countered sardonically, knuckles on his hips. "He's not able to stand on his feet for a long time. Well. Well. Well." Thick glasses stared in utter disbelief at the prisoners lined up. Then turning back to Mr. Weiss, the SS man fumed, "And *now*, now he thinks he can" – he paused a moment, groping for the proper word – "can do what he wants? And he thinks that that is all right with us?"

Enraged, both arms crossed over his chest, the colonel placed his feet apart and glared at the older Weiss in utter fury and contempt.

No one moved. Everyone remained silent.

"*Nein, Herr Obersturmführer*" (No, Sir), Weiss ventured diffidently. *Herr Obersturmführer*, my foot.

My mind drifts back to the camp when I think of those words, "*Herr Obersturmführer*" or "*Herr Oberscharführer*." It makes me think of the Nazis' rigid obedience and the obsequiousness of Nazi soldiers

standing at ramrod attention, obediently clicking their heels and raising their hands in holy salute. It would have been laughable, had they
not been capable of such devastating destruction.

"Very well," Weber said crisply. "I think that is what he thinks.
Well," he continued, still fuming with rage, "we'll see. We'll see."

The SS officer turned to his subordinates standing submissively
like squatting birds in the rain and spoke to them briefly. Turning back,
he gave us a five-minute angry speech about how he was going to make
an example of malingering prisoners.

Actually, that night as the previous nights, the prisoners had seriously advised De Witt not to anger the SS any longer and told him
he'd better report to roll call. They'd argued that beyond punishing De
Witt himself, the SS in their fury would punish the entire barracks and
would withdraw their pitiful bread rations in retaliation for De Witt's
maddening stubbornness.

But in vain.

De Witt remained adamant and decided not to attend roll call
again. He refused to listen, stubborn like a mule. He had lain on his
bunk, arms behind his head, eyes glaring madly at us. "Get out," he
had growled gruffly, "and leave me alone!" There was no way to make
the man listen to reason.

The next day, the SS found him comfortably lying on his bunk in
the barracks, stubbornly refusing to attend roll call.

This time the SS meant business. This time they were not going to
monkey around. They definitely were going to make an example out of
this man and show us what happened to someone who didn't comply
with SS orders.

We were ordered to line up in ranks of five in the numbing cold in
the roll call square.

We waited. No one moved. No one spoke a word.

Bull-necked commandant Josef Kramer stepped into the barracks
where De Witt was resting, accompanied by two husky SS *Scharführers*

armed with wooden billy clubs and side arms and SS guard Lukas Pavlenko with a fearsome-looking iron bar.

Half a dozen tough muscled *Kapos* and SS-Totenkopfverbände (Death's Head Units) armed with Mauser rifles and pistols stood spaced along the barbed-wire fence near the gate surrounding us for any "eventualities." One of the *Häftlinge* (prisoners) standing in the row behind me whispered, "What do they think they're doing? Do they believe we skeletons are going to attack them so they can kill all of us?"

The SS stood there across from us with flat, no-nonsense looks on their impassive faces, hands on their guns, and waited. And we waited.

Several minutes went by. Then we could hear a hoarse howl coming through the open door of De Witt's barracks. And then a groan. Then a scream. Then we heard the snarling voices of SS officers and the sound of falling clubs coming from the barracks. Then we heard blubbering, muffled this time.

These Nazis guys were not kidding. De Witt, this young enfeebled man, was not going to survive such a murderous, vicious assault.

The beatings and the snarling voices went on for a couple of minutes.

Then the barracks door opened, and the five men stepped outside. This scene stayed with me, imprinted on my mind. De Witt, led by the two grim-looking SS *Scharführer*s, came out of the barracks, followed by unfazed commandant Kramer and young, impassive-faced Pavlenko. De Witt's face was barely recognizable. One eye was swollen shut, his lips were grossly enlarged, and blood came out of his mouth whenever he coughed. He had difficulty walking straight. They had beaten the living daylights out of him with either a wooden club or the iron bar, or perhaps the walnut butt of one of their rifles.

Small wonder they hadn't dragged De Witt into the open square and shot him (as a deterrent to other recalcitrants) in front of us.

Obviously the SS were satisfied showing us how they were going to deal with any insubordinate behavior in the camp.

Later De Witt told us that Pavlenko had hit him in the head with the wooden club over and over as his cohorts stood there watching him hum a Lithuanian tune while he was inflicting this savage beating.

We stood there lined up in columns of fives. De Witt, barely able to stand up straight, was being held by his arms by two fellow prisoners.

The four SS officers, looking very pleased with themselves, started the recount. They worked their way methodically through the line of prisoners, counting each one meticulously until they came to De Witt. All four stood back to admire their handiwork.

"*Na schön*, very well," said SS Obersturmführer Weber amiably, turning away from De Witt, looking steely-eyed at all the inmates standing near him. "I hope this will teach you prisoners to obey our orders."

De Witt, supported by the two prisoners, stood in silence, slightly rocking back and forth on his heels, staring dreamily at the SS man as though listening to the sound of some distant music. Then suddenly, giggling idiotically, he threw his head back and let out a roar of uncontrolled, maniacal laughter.

Caught up short, Obersturmführer Weber gazed at him dumbfounded.

De Witt stopped his hysterical laughter and then, simply grinning provocatively at the officers, he contemptuously spat out a tooth at one of the officer's feet, and a new bout of convulsive coughing shook De Witt and more blood poured from his mouth, spotting his jacket.

Weber looked at De Witt and then glanced about at the other prisoners, not really knowing what to do next, whether to draw his pistol and shoot De Witt point-blank in the face or beat him with the iron bar he was still carrying. He shook his head, perhaps concluding the guy was a complete lunatic. Then the SS officer walked down the line of prisoners, the other SS apes following him obediently.

When the call "*Wegtreten*" (Dismissed) was sounded, and both fellow prisoners let go of De Witt's arms, he collapsed as though he'd been kicked in the back of his knees.

Everybody dispersed except for two prisoners who waited with De Witt a few minutes more until two inmates arrived from the hospital. They took his arms and guided him, hobbling, across the square toward the hospital barracks.

A week after De Witt was taken to the hospital ward, I woke up in the middle of the night to a brief series of machine-gun bursts. German voices were calling out a warning. We couldn't make out what it was all about, but we knew for sure something bad had happened.

When stillness fell, a few prisoners went looking outside in the black night. They came back without having seen anything abnormal.

The next morning at daybreak, we learned that De Witt had been shot dead.

When the labor detachments got lined up in the gray dawn light, they saw him hanging in a grotesque lifeless position, entangled in the barbed-wire fence.

He looked like he'd been crucified. Nobody knew for sure what happened. Rumor had it that in the dead of the night, De Witt in his deteriorating condition had slipped out of the hospital and was seen talking to an SS guard outside the hospital barracks.

When he was about to make a dash across the deserted grounds toward the barbed-wire fence, guards in the watch tower who intermittently swept their blinding searchlights across the square caught him seconds away from leaping at the electrified barbed wire, barked commands – which fell on deaf ears – and opened up, riddling him with bullets.

The SS staff had left his body hanging in the double wire fence as a warning to all prisoners.

However it happened, we speculated, he had tried to escape, or what seemed more logical, had gone off the deep end and committed suicide.

It was later that we found out that De Witt had been suffering from severe tuberculosis. It didn't matter, really.

In the end, the man had found his peace.

SEVENTEEN

The Last Yards

Bergen-Belsen camp – early March 1945.

The camp oven was working overtime; dead bodies were piled on top of each other. Everything that happened seemed haphazard – whether you lived or died, were lucky or unlucky, it looked like a throw of the dice.

The camp was overflowing with a tsunami of prisoners evacuated mainly from Auschwitz.

During those bitter latter days, tempers would explode. People had become cold, inconsiderate, and quarrelsome. Everyone looked out for his own interests. Everybody. It was a zero-sum game – it's either me or else it's you who stands or falls, like two boxers fighting in the ring for the championship. Usually the stronger one wins and the weaker one loses, but it's *you* who *wants* to win, it's you who keeps throwing hard punches, keeps jabbing and feinting, throwing a hook or a crossing right, hoping to get the title. You want to *survive*, that's what counts, *survive at all costs*.

During this time, many prisoners reached a point of weakness of not being able to walk about. I imagine they thought that soon the crematorium would be their next stop, that freedom would never be theirs. I could see these desperate men and women hanging on to life by their fingernails.

Despair hovered over Bergen-Belsen, an ugly storm cloud that signaled whatever was up ahead would be even worse. Hopelessness invaded everyone, including the guards, because Germany was losing the war, and Nazis would soon be called to answer for their hideous crimes.

When it came to food distribution, tempers exploded. Frequently there were quarrels – often between secular and observant Jews, who weren't particularly fond of each other.

I recall one day a large metal container filled with kohlrabi soup arrived unexpectedly in our barracks from the camp kitchen, and prisoners rushed at it like a wild mob at Macy's Black Friday sale.

Some of the prisoners would wait out the rush and stand at the end of the line. Generally, the guy who would ladle the soup into our bowls wouldn't stir enough, and naturally, the soup would get thicker toward the bottom of the pot. Prisoners standing at the end of the line would get more cabbage than those who were standing up front. The latter would get miffed about it and shout out loud: "Hey, you, holy ones! Waiting for some thicker soup, eh? Don't stand there and wait, get in line like everyone else, *vroome rotkop*, pious knuckleheads!"

People who were subjected to starvation and had been degraded by the humiliating life in the camp would stoop that low. Sadly, even in these horrific living conditions, people would stick to biased opinions. Non-believers would keep mocking: "Where is your God now?" and observant people would keep replying: "Only God will keep us alive now."

Occasionally, emotions would erupt in an ugly fit of abuse and derogatory name calling. Many scenes of such debasing slurs are stuck in my mind.

I remember after one such ugly, unruly fight between the two groups, I walked out of the barracks and saw a man – a boy, really, maybe sixteen years old – bending over a large food container, scraping and scraping and scraping with a metal spoon, hoping to find some leftovers at the bottom of the pot. But as usual, the scraping had been in vain; the container was totally empty. And now he moved to other containers standing outside the barracks waiting to be brought back to the kitchen and started scraping their bottoms, scraped and scraped like a madman, and finally, with a hopeless gesture, threw the spoon away, slid down the wall of the barracks, and sat on the ground with his arms wrapped around his knees, gazing over them into the emptiness with desolate eyes.

There he sat, mouth slightly open, staring mutely into space, starved, hardly looking human at all, a forlorn figure, forgotten by the world.

And that is called *hunger*.

That image, indelibly seared into my brain all those decades ago, instantly reawakens the memories of hunting for food, *any kind* of food, even potato peels, even leftovers that in another life we would carelessly have discarded, absolutely anything edible. We daydreamed about food. Eventually, we had hallucinations of food, succulent steaks dancing before our feverish eyes. And we kept hoping…

The advance of the Allied forces in Western Europe was making rapid progress, and we could hear combat aircraft flying overhead above the clouds. The distant rattling machine-gun fire was growing nearer, and the old motto was heard more than ever: "*Keep it up; tough it out.*"

The always optimistically smiling Mr. Weiss reassured us that the rumors passing back and forth were true; a breakthrough might come very soon. The possibility that soon we might walk out through the gates as free people gave us fresh hope.

There was talk around the tables that the Nazis were ready to create diplomatic channels to open negotiations for a separate peace with the Western Allies, and we would be exchanged for Germans held in British or US territories in return for *goods* and hard *cash. Hard cash?* All right.

If the Nazis wanted cash, then maybe soon we might get out of here.

And then rumors began to circulate that Berlin had sent direct orders to the SS-Hauptamt that all inmates were to be eliminated rather than have them fall into the hands of the enemy. Hearing this shocking news struck a cold blade of terror into us.

"Any truth to these reports?" we asked Weiss, running into him outside of the barracks.

He shook his head. "Nonsense. How do you suppose they can do this? Forty thousand prisoners and tens of thousands more pouring in from the east every day?" He shook his head again. "Be sensible. Besides, the Germans know that the war is lost. No, no," he reassured us, pausing at the barracks entrance. "If this were true, I would know about it."

And we kept trudging along like stubborn men and women wearily slogging through heavy rains, mud and storms, day in and day out, hoping to survive, knowing the storm eventually will pass over and lose steam. But after each day's storm passed, a new black ominous one loomed up ahead. We clenched our teeth and kept plodding on, not giving up, hoping that this one would be the last one, the final one. And in that spirit, we lived. Westerbork came to mind; were people burying their heads in the sand again?

Then one morning, the roll calls ground to a complete halt.

Too many prisoners were dying. Who was going to count the corpses lying sprawled on floors in the barracks?

Not long after, Vader's health took a bad turn.

PART THREE

Are We Free Yet?

EIGHTEEN

Waiting

My daily morning routine during those weeks in March consisted of getting up together with the grownups before they went off to work and heading to the freezing sanitary facility to wash beneath the open taps of the row of steel sinks. After that, and after drinking the brown liquid called coffee and wolfing down the slice of bread (we still obtained our food rations at the time), I made my bed in proper military style (*you'd better pay attention, boy, and make sure that the corners of the blanket are tucked in as tightly as they can be underneath the straw mattress*).

This was followed by the sickening task (which often made me want to throw up) of checking the seams of my shirt, my undershirt, and my pajamas for any wingless lice that might be crawling around there. The kids in the camp who weren't sick would start sweeping the floors with frayed straw brooms.

There was great relief among the prisoners when we first heard the rumor that the Allied forces were fighting their way into the heartland of Germany. But my father's mood was not heightened by the news. During this period, I watched him slowly change from a relatively healthy person to a gravely ill man.

I was not fully aware of the debilitating condition Vader had been suffering from. I would watch him going off to work. Like all of us, he was skeletal, his once large, stocky frame now bent and emaciated. He had a slight limp from who knows what altercation or run-in with the wrong guard. The worst part was the change in his face. Once lively and expressive, it now bore a blank, almost detached expression, which I was not able to read.

One morning, I talked to Moeder about it. With her eyes fixed on mine, she confirmed my anxiety and said, "I don't like it at all the way he looks and acts."

The gravity of Vader's condition became evident the day he stayed in the barracks and didn't go to work.

The next day, his face was flushed with fever, his skin was blotchy, and he had a racking cough.

It was unbearable to think that the British forces (according to Mr. Weiss) were battling the Germans practically on the doorstep of the camp now, and we soon would be free, but Vader was falling victim, as many others had, to a frighteningly debilitating disease known as hunger edema.

I felt my heart sink within me. *Please, please, no.*

I was terribly afraid we would miss out again like on that terrible morning when SS Aufseherin Krumm with a cold shrug had refused to let us board the trucks to freedom. *Not again. Not again experiencing this bitter irony, this injustice, this pointlessness. Please, no.* I refused to think about it.

This time, I told myself, *Vader will be okay. He will be lucky. He will be all right. Of course, he will. We need to get out of here.*

The next morning, his condition hadn't changed.

I sat down at his bedside and asked, "How is it going, Papa?" (I still can see the scene in my head, almost can hear the dialogue). He shot me a weak smile. "I'm good, son. I'm doing fine. I'll be all right." A racking cough shook his body.

I sat and waited. Then he told me, "Your two brothers came to see me yesterday evening after they got back from work." I nodded. I didn't see them in the morning. They had left early for work and lived in another barracks.

In general, as strange as it sounds, my brothers and I didn't see much of each other. They went to work, were gone all day, had their circle of friends, and the only time we saw each other was at "supper" at the table in the barracks. When we talked, our conversations were limited because they were exhausted. That's the way the days went by in the camp – just enduring.

I had often heard people say that willpower can work wonders, and I was struck by an idea: maybe there was a way to lift Vader's spirits.

I turned to him. "Papa, we learned from Joop Weiss that the Allied forces are battling the Nazis and are practically on the doorstep of the camp. Everybody expects the war soon to be over."

"Really?" he said, his eyes lighting up like candles in a cathedral.

"Yes," I replied, nodding encouragingly.

"Well," he smiled weakly, "that's good, very good."

He didn't believe me. It was plainly written, like a billboard, across his face.

Another cough shook his body.

When he stopped coughing, he turned his head slowly, stared across at me with a weak smile, and said, "I don't dare think that I might be so lucky as to get out of this miserable, filthy, death-ridden place alive. Ever since the day that Nazi woman refused to allow us to get onto the truck, something inside me changed. It felt like the whole world fell apart. I don't believe anymore. I don't think I'll get out of this place alive."

He gave a hopeless sigh, and we were both silent, thinking about that unforgettable nightmarish day.

We had been so close to freedom, and then *bam*, like a bolt out of the blue, everything suddenly had changed, with the casual wave of a Nazi's hand. And now Vader was lying here, emotionally shattered, demolished like a smashed house after an air strike, without hope, without any resolve, and because the strength of will he had possessed before had left him now, his condition was deteriorating rapidly.

I thought for a moment. What else would encourage him to hang in there?

"We'll soon be free, Papa," I said lamely. I nodded. "Very soon."

"Yes," he said, "that's good, very good."

"Aren't you glad, Papa?" I asked, watching him curiously.

"Yes, I am." He looked up and asked, "Could you bring me a cup of coffee, please?"

A cup of coffee? I thought. *What cup of coffee? From where?*

"Of course, Papa," I said, though as I got up, I was thinking, *Where in this hellhole do I get a cup of coffee?* "I'll be right back."

I went to look for Weiss and found him in one of the barracks talking to a prisoner. I approached him, excused myself for interrupting, and told him about Vader's wish.

Joop Weiss turned to me, nodded his gray head gravely and looked me in the eye. "Your father needs to be hospitalized," he said. "He can't lie there like this. He needs to be under a doctor's supervision."

I stared at him blankly. *What doctor?* I hadn't seen a doctor in a long time.

"I noted his condition making my sick report to the SS staff. You know, the roll calls."

"There haven't been roll calls lately," I told him.

"Nevertheless, I need to make my reports. They're still checking the work details."

Of course. "Is there somewhere I can get some coffee for my papa?"

Weiss looked off for a moment. "Yes," he said, "there's still some coffee around somewhere." He paused a moment. "Wait here."

Five minutes later, he came back, holding the cup of colored liquid in his hand. "I'm really sorry," he told me, handing it to me. "About your father."

I walked with the cupful of "coffee" back to our barracks and brought it to my father's bunk.

Meanwhile Moeder had come by and sat there talking to him, giving him a pep talk. But he lay there motionless, eyes closed. She took the cup from me and, leaning forward, said, "Look what Wolfi has brought you, Ephraim."

He opened his eyes for a moment, drank a few swallows from the cup, looked at me, smiled, and said, "Yes, thank you, son."

We sat for a little while longer with Vader and tried to cheer him up. He lay there listlessly with his eyes closed. Every now and then he would nod his head, but otherwise he kept silent. The symptoms of hunger edema were all too familiar to me, and my heart felt heavy.

All around us there was silence.

To distract my mind, I went outside to take a breath of fresh air.

It was windy, and the ground was covered with two inches of snow. Huddling deep in my thin winter overcoat, I took deep breaths and looked around me.

Everything looked white, and the snowflakes kept falling silently on my hair and face, whirling around me in gusts of wind.

I spotted the stiff body of a dead prisoner lying half hidden beneath the blanket of snow. His hand was thrust out as though he had been begging for mercy. For a long moment I could not take my eyes off the body. Then I turned and spotted more twisted bodies, lying there like thrown-away junk. I was surrounded by death.

These prisoners most likely went out of the barracks to get a breath of fresh air just as I had. They must have dropped from sheer starvation, their malnourished bodies unable to hold them up. The snow and the silence enhanced the gruesomeness of that creepy sight.

I was about to go back to the barracks when I heard the muffled sound of a motor. I turned. An open truck of the crematoria detail was pulling up, and three gravediggers, still looking to be in relatively good shape (due to their extra food ration), climbed down and with shovels and makeshift stretchers started to collect the dead.

I remember standing there for a long minute watching with almost rapt fascination as they loaded the dead like a heap of garbage upon the roofless lorry.

Once their job was done, they swung up and drove off through the thickening curtain of falling snowflakes.

I looked after them for a moment and then turned and headed back toward my barracks, wondering what the next few days would bring.

NINETEEN

~

The Hospital Ward

It was a midweek day in late March 1945 when Vader was admitted to the hospital ward. When I entered the hospital barracks, Vader was in a narrow room lying on a mattress with a filthy, ripped-up sheet covering the peeling iron bed. If memory serves me correctly, he was there alone, and there were no bunks in there. A kind of sickly sweet odor filled the room.

I drew up a chair and sat there staring at him.

"Hi, Papa," I said.

He turned his head slightly and said in a feeble voice from the bed, "Hi, Wolf."

I leaned forward closer toward him and asked, "How are you feeling?"

He didn't respond, simply gave a resigned smile and closed his eyes.

I really didn't need to hear any answer. What I saw told me enough. He was suffering a disease known as hunger edema. The blunt diagnosis of the doctor whom Moeder had consulted had not been very encouraging. I can still see him ticking the symptoms off on his little finger: swelling of the joints, skin rashes, organ damage, loss of muscle mass, heart failure.

This awful disease spread across Nazi camps with alarming speed. He was lying motionless, and his breathing was labored. Two

94

drab-colored corduroy blankets covered his body, and his bloated belly protruded under them.

I found myself staring at it. There was a moment's silence.

He turned to me. "Mr. Weiss got me here."

I nodded. Good old Joop Weiss.

"He told me the Allies are closing in on the camp."

"That's right, Papa. Who knows, maybe in a couple of days, you know." I recalled that I had said the same thing a couple of days before, and I felt like a broken record.

"Well, yes, you are right, maybe in a couple of days."

He stared blankly into space, quietly closed his eyes again, and lapsed into silence.

As I sat there, something crossed my mind: I hadn't seen either a doctor or a nurse for some time now. Where could they be?

I leaned close. "Have you seen a doctor, Papa?"

He opened his eyes and shook his head no.

No nurses? No doctors? I thought. *Who looks after the sick, then?*

Vader moved his head. "Can you get me some water, please? I feel dehydrated." His voice sounded hoarse. Dehydration, I was told, was another symptom of the disease.

I nodded. "Yes, of course." I rose to get Vader some water. But the water supply had stopped, and as I stood there, hoping to find some, a young nurse dressed in a grimy white dress hurried by. I asked her if she could get some water for Vader. The woman paused, threw a quick a glance at my father, nodded, and was already on her way out the door when I added that Vader hadn't seen any doctor. She stopped, glanced at my silent father again, and then, her face subtly veiled, said to me, "Don't worry, yes? A doctor will be here soon." She nodded, gave me a faint smile, and walked off.

I looked after her and thought to myself, *from her lips to God's ear.*

Vader said from the bed, "Thank you, son."

A couple of minutes later, the nurse smilingly handed me a cupful of water. She waited and looked on for a moment as Vader slowly raised himself – with my help – and took a few slow swallows. Then handing the cup back to me, he laid his head back down on the pillow, turned to look at me, said something like "You're a good son," and closed his eyes.

I sat there silently at Vader's bedside and flashed back to the years before the camp. Did I ever even really know my father? Did he ever really know me?

My parents had witnessed Hitler's rise to power and went through the nightmares of racial persecution. Their lives had been turned upside down, and regular family bonding was a luxury we never had. In those years, the values that included family were downplayed. Under the new German civilian administration in the Netherlands, everything was geared toward honoring the Führer – and toward persecution of the Jews.

After a while, I got up, went down the ward, stepped carefully around the dead bodies lying sprawled on the floor, went outside, and made my way across the snowy grounds back to the freezing barracks, where I hoped to find Weiss.

I met him in the rear of the barracks and thanked him for taking care of Vader.

There was a stern expression on Weiss's face. "Your father *has* to be under a physician's supervision."

I hesitated. "But there are no doctors."

He gave me a reassuring nod. "There will be." He paused a moment. "But the situation might soon take a turn for the worse."

"How do you mean?"

Weiss gave a shrug. He turned to look at other prisoners who had moved closer to listen. He confirmed that the trucks carrying medical supplies had been bombarded. "The plant that has been pumping out drinking water for the camp was bombarded." He sighed. "Everything seems on the verge of collapse." He added, "I am completely powerless. Hopefully the Allied troops will soon reach the camp."

It was a distressing situation. Vader was lying there helpless, and Weiss had apparently no medical supply at his disposal. Everything had stopped like a stalled engine in the desert, and contagious diseases were spreading like wildfire. The SS and *Kapos* were nowhere to be seen. Like wounded animals, they had crawled away into hidden holes trying to save themselves from the expected Allied onslaught.

After the war, we learned the truth: the SS had deliberately misled us in a most cunning way. At the Lüneburg tribunal in Lower Saxony, also called the Belsen Trial (the defendants put on trial were camp commandant Josef Kramer and men and women of the SS who had worked at Auschwitz and Bergen-Belsen), British Brigadier Llewelyn Glynn Hughes testified that on April 5, 1945, a British armored division had come across a Wehrmacht (German armed forces) camp, one mile north of the Bergen-Belsen camp complex, fully stocked with an abundance of food; they found over fifty thousand loaves of bread, thousands of cans of meat and milk, and an amassed stack of Red Cross parcels that had been sent by loving family members for the prisoners (all stolen and withheld by the SS), plus vast quantities of medical supplies. The Brits discovered the Bergen-Belsen water system had been running properly with full water and sanitation, but the SS staff had simply malevolently sabotaged it.

Meanwhile, we were desperate. As the Red Army advanced west, the enormous flood of prisoners arriving daily in open-topped freight cars from Auschwitz and other camps further east kept pouring in unabated. Our camp, called the Sternlager (Star Camp), for our yellow stars, soon swarmed with the new arrivals. These newcomers were seen wandering ghostlike about the camp grounds, covered with blankets to keep themselves protected from the freezing cold. The SS people had put them in makeshift tents without bunks or lighting and with nothing but some thin layers of straw on the ground. They had no food or water.

I often find myself reliving those days. There was one striking element amid the chaos and despair and deterioration: an uncommon look on many survivors' faces, a determined teeth-gritting expression, an absolute rock hard resolve and willpower to survive these final days of agonizing wretchedness.

This look was missing from my father's face. I noticed that immediately when I went to visit him that morning. My father's swollen face reflected nothing but a resigned apathy, a clear sign that he was gradually sinking into a slow, dream-like comatose state. He didn't seem to perceive – *didn't seem to mind* anymore – what was going on around him. Did a doctor come to see him? I don't know. I don't think so. I never found out. What I saw was that his condition had rapidly changed for the worse. Vader just lay there now, didn't move, barely was able to breathe. The other prisoners moving around us ignored his condition completely. No one gave a damn.

And as I sat by Vader's bedside, may the Lord forgive me, I didn't feel a thing. Nothing. Maybe it was because of all the death and squalor around me. Constantly seeing people die from disease, from random punishments, and from starvation, I had become hardened to the suffering of others – including my father's.

Moeder arrived at the hospital. Her work details had been discontinued. She stood motionless and studied Vader's face in silence. She took a slow step forward and called out softly, "Ephraim…can you hear me?"

There was no answer, only a screaming silence. I realized my father was in a coma. She called his name again, watching him intently. Maybe a couple of seconds went by. Moeder looked across at me with such anguish in her eyes that I sat rooted to my chair. She stood for a moment silently watching him, then turned and went out the door, as quick as a shot.

When my thoughts turn to those days, all the frustration and anguish we experienced during the years in the camp pours over me. I picture Vader lying there on the bed, and I am engulfed in hopelessness. Fury gushes over me like a spouting hose, filling me with such bitterness that I want to yell at the top of my voice against the unfairness of it all. How did I end up seated at my father's death bed in a concentration camp just before the war was over?

My eyes rested on him, and I whispered shakily, "Please, Papa, stay with us. Please, Papa, don't die on us, please."

TWENTY

~

Surely the End Must Come Soon

It must have been two days later, after midnight on the second night of Passover in March 1945, that I woke up to the glare of a flashlight shining in my eyes.

I slowly sat up and saw the dark outline of a tall figure in a threadbare coat standing in front of my bunk. I recognized the man; he was the Blockälteste's assistant, a young Dutchman. I rubbed my eyes trying to figure out what was going on and drowsily asked, "What's up? What happened, Decker?"

He hesitated for a moment.

"*Je vader is overleden, jongen*," he said. "Your father has passed away. One hour ago."

It took a moment to sink in.

His bony hand patted my arm. "I'm sorry."

Slowly I slid off the middle bunk to the floor.

The Dutchman lingered for a moment. "You okay?"

I looked up and nodded.

I had expected it to happen, but not that way, not that soon. When the message hits you, it's like a vicious punch to the stomach. It staggers you.

"Have you told this to my mother, or to anyone –"

He shook his head. "To nobody." He paused a moment. "I think you'd better get dressed. Someone else is going to come here," he said. "He'll take care of it." He patted me on the shoulder and then turned and walked down the length of the room out the door and into the night.

Now it was up to me to tell Moeder. I got dressed slowly, stretching out the task so I could delay the moment when I would have to say the words to her. I glanced at the watch my parents had given me on my birthday in better times. It was 3:25 on the luminous dial.

Around me was deep silence. People were asleep. No one, I guessed, had heard us talking. While I got dressed, I thought about what was going on at the hospital ward right now. The scenes were acutely familiar to me; I had experienced them more than once while sitting at my father's bedside. First off, there would be the authoritarian voice of a nurse calling out that whoever had died should be quickly taken away, claiming they needed more space to make room for new patients.

More unsettling thoughts passed through my head when another curly-headed, bony-faced young man in a black sweater and gabardine trousers appeared at my bunk. "Holles?" he asked guardedly. "Wolf Holles?"

I nodded yes.

He motioned for me to follow him. "Come along." He was, I guessed, one of the men who belonged to the burial detail.

I eyed him. "What about my two brothers?"

He frowned. "Your brothers? What about them?"

"I thought that they should also know."

He gave a shrug and said that Weiss had told him to tell just me.

In the big chaos in the camp, my brothers had recently been moved to another barracks, and I even didn't know where they were.

I felt something drop inside me. "All right," I said. "I will go alone."

"Good." He glanced at his watch and then looked up. "Let's go."

"Yes," I said. "Okay."

I felt a chill, and my stomach clenched.

I put on my thin overcoat, and we walked in the heavy silence through the sleeping barracks and stepped through the door out into the whistling wet night. I shivered. Sleet and freezing rain beat down upon us like fists as we made our way across the deserted assembly ground past the silent barracks toward the hospital ward.

I bowed my head into the driving, biting wind, following the man mechanically. After a five-minute walk through the wet darkness across the muddy grounds, we arrived at the one-story low-slung hospital barracks. Two dim lights shone in a small, wood-framed window. The man opened the door and I followed him inside. My heart started bouncing around like a ping-pong ball. The man was sensitive enough not to talk; he didn't say a word. A heavy, rancid odor permeated the ward. A nurse wearing a white jacket rushed like a ghost past us in the semi-darkness, talking over her shoulder. I almost tripped over the body of a sick prisoner lying on his back on a mattress on the floor.

At the far end of the ward, a second, younger man with closely cropped blond hair stood waiting beside my father's bunk. A stretcher was positioned on the stony floor beside the iron bed beneath a dangling bare bulb.

I looked at Vader lying there on the narrow bed, his body half covered with a soiled, torn sheet. His face looked changed. The man lying there was a stranger, yet it *was* my father. I felt a hollow sickness lurching in my chest. Here was my father – I had been talking to him only one day ago, and now he was gone.

Now as I stood there, the tears wouldn't come. I remember the only feeling I had was a cold chill shooting up my spine.

I watched the man with the blond crew cut hand me the few humble things that had once belonged to Vader: a threadbare brown winter jacket, a pair of dark-framed eyeglasses, a Swiss watch that had stopped, and a crumpled, yellowed wallet that had nothing in it.

One of the odd things about the Star Camp was that the SS had been *generous* with regard to personal effects. We were allowed to hold on to such things as my father's broken watch and useless leather wallet.

They were kind enough to allow us to keep such tokens. But I regarded these few items indifferently. These things, now that Vader was gone, were dead objects to me.

Moments later, we started off.

The blond one nodded his head toward his companion, and they put Vader down on the stretcher on the floor and covered him with the filthy sheet. Without saying a word, they lifted the gurney with my papa on it, stepped through the door, and moved into the windy, misty night.

I followed them, silent.

They stopped walking for a moment and the curly-headed fellow with the bony face who had come to fetch me said to me, "Meneer Weiss wanted me to inform you." He paused a moment. "Was he a friend of your father?"

I nodded. "Yes, they went way back."

Before they continued, the curly-headed one gave me a sideways glance and said awkwardly, "You may want to come along."

I nodded silently.

We walked along the rows of silent barracks toward the deserted, dark assembly square through the freezing rain and sleet that kept pounding us, the two men carrying Vader on the gurney and I his meager belongings. And this was how I escorted Vader on his last journey.

A few minutes later, we arrived at a small lean-to shed with a sloping, leaking metal roof. The two men stopped, put down the rain-soaked stretcher with my father on it, turned to me, and waited.

I knew what was inside the shed; I knew the nude corpses that were stacked up like cords of wood would be dumped into open ditches or hauled off by trailers to the incinerator. I stood a moment and then realized that the two wanted to spare me watching the grisly sight of them rolling Vader off the stretcher and then flinging his body like a piece of trash upon the heap. And believe me, as God is my witness, I had already seen more of these sights than I ever wanted to. Without saying a word, I turned around with my father's possessions and slowly headed for my mother's barracks. To this day, I have never understood why I, as a young boy, was called to Vader after he had succumbed to starvation and not my mother or my older brothers.

Plodding my way through the cold night, a fleeting thought entered my mind: there had been no minyan to say the Kaddish for my father, the Jewish prayer for the dead.

Now I was about to face Moeder. It was a short walk to her barracks. I walked as slowly as possible.

TWENTY-ONE

Relaying Bitter News

A cold wind swept through the dark night across the Belsen camp. In a few minutes, I reached Moeder's barracks.

Inside, everybody was asleep.

Slowly, I approached her bunk. My heart was beating in my throat. How was I going to explain to her about Vader? She was asleep when I reached her bed. After a moment's hesitation, I reached out and lightly touched her arm and stood waiting.

She woke up with a start, looked around with confused eyes, and then, seeing me, quickly raised herself on her elbow. Instantly alarmed, she pushed herself upright, brushed a strand of hair out her face, took my hand, and our eyes locked. "What *happened*, Wolfi?"

I could see fear in her eyes.

I took a deep breath. "Mama, it's Papa. He died this morning."

"No, no," she said. "No, no." She shook her head from side to side. "No, no." Tears filled her eyes.

"They killed him!" she began to cry softly, her voice choking. "The m-monsters murdered him!"

And then she wept.

I stood there and swallowed.

Around us people woke up and soon sorrowful sighs followed when they found out what the crying was about.

"Tell me everything." She grabbed on to my hand and began to sob.

I withdrew my hand slowly so that I could think without becoming too emotional. I tried hard to speak clearly.

God knows, there was no need to say much. While listening to me, she let out a stifled sob. "Oh, my God, why?"

As I sat there looking at her, a memory flashed in my mind. I saw that SS guard brutally striking Moeder, savagely beating her with that hardwood truncheon, like a close-up shot on a movie screen.

That mental image would haunt me for a long time. Yet I knew Vader's death hurt her more than that beating.

As Moeder sat there wiping her eyes with her hands, trying hard to regain her composure, I placed Vader's things at the foot of her bed, then took off my wet coat and sat down on the edge of the bunk bed. I sat there silent for a long moment. I wanted to say some words of comfort to her, but nothing came out.

I marveled at my cold detachment. Was this how my friends felt while we joked about the foods we would eat? I wouldn't know. I never talked to them about it – all we talked about was food over and over and all the things we wanted to do after the liberation. We felt sick and wanted to leave, leave this killing place, and be with people who lived without fear, in a place where there was laughter, a warm home and safe haven. We just wanted to enjoy doing the things we used to do in our former free lives.

Clinging to these thoughts, I closed my eyes for a long moment and found myself back in the sunny Dutch seaside resort of Scheveningen, where we used to spend our summer vacation. I could suddenly see the bumper boats and the thrilling water slide, the whirring carousels and the festooned arcades and cafés where the crowd sat and chatted and drank at little tables that ran out to the edge of the sidewalks. I could see the dazzling whiteness of the sandy beach and remember its perpetual strong scent of salty sea air. Most of all, I was swept up by the feeling of being *free*. What would it be like to live without the dreadful, awful feeling of being in captivity? To hell with all this misery.

I opened my eyes and took a deep breath. We sat in silence for a few more minutes.

I shivered. The cold of the icy wind outside had seeped into my bones, and I wrapped my jacket tightly around me.

Moeder looked at me. "We must be strong."

I nodded.

"We'll get through this, Wolfi."

"Yes, Mama."

Her voice began to crumble. She wiped her eyes and tucked a strand of her hair behind her ear.

"You'd better get back to your barracks now and get some sleep."

I nodded. "Okay, Mama." I got up. "Are you all right?"

"Yes, I'm – I'm fine."

We both knew that nothing was fine.

After I said goodnight to Moeder and slunk back outside into the freezing rain and sleet, I stood there for a long moment on the muddy ground listening to the steady droning sound of the Allied planes that were flying overhead high above the clouds. *How much longer?*

TWENTY-TWO

Evacuation: The Beginning of the End?

In early April, rumors started floating around the camp that again exchange prisoners were going to be evacuated.

The first transport with "exchange" Jews, mostly Dutch, had left the camp on January 20 without us. We would never forget that date. But maybe now it really was our turn to leave.

The rumors that kept floating around raised the tension. Especially now, as we all sensed the war was drawing to a close.

We waited impatiently to hear the good news.

Meanwhile, everywhere as far as the eye could see, there was deterioration, deterioration, and more deterioration. No roll calls anymore, no *Arbeitskommandos* leaving the camp, and everywhere we turned, there was abject wretchedness: filth, sticky muck and diseases, hollow-cheeked, starved prisoners shuffling about like scarecrows, little smudge-faced children wailing from hunger, desperate mothers lifting their hands, rolling their eyes to the heavens praying for absolution.

And the icy North German wind kept cutting right through our bones while the unsanitary state in the camp made our blood curdle. And to top it all off, the new rumor that the SS were going to liquidate the camp and execute all the inmates hung over us like a static black cloud.

Then things began to move fast.

The rumors that had been swirling around Bergen-Belsen the past couple of days were now confirmed. We exchange prisoners – those who held South American documents – were about to leave the camp.

As British troops were advancing on the camp, the SS made special efforts to evacuate as many prisoners as possible from Bergen-Belsen.

I can vividly recall that day; it was a bleak, gloomy morning, and a dense, low-flying fog was like gray smoke drifting over the camp.

The night before, there had been a sudden flurry of excitement; prisoners were milling about frantically, carrying suitcases, bags, and cardboard cartons tied with ropes. The next morning, we stood outside excitedly talking to one another, waiting near the barracks for the trucks to arrive and drive us to a nearby loading platform.

Two trains had already left the camp, the first on April 6, and the second one, made up of largely Hungarian prisoners, on April 7. The third train was scheduled to leave the camp with twenty-five hundred prisoners on April 11. My family and I were scheduled to be on it. Rumors kept circulating about the end of the war. It would be the last transport leaving Bergen-Belsen.

The previous day, we had caught sight of Josef Weiss standing outside the barracks nearest to the gate talking to a group of prisoners. Moeder and I joined the group.

Mr. Weiss apparently was about to board one of the trucks with us. As always, he kept his friendly calm and answered all our questions precisely. It had been Mr. Weiss who had ordered us to gather our meager belongings and get ready to leave. He had informed us that about twenty-five hundred prisoners would leave the camp.

Where are they sending us?" Moeder wanted to know.

"Czechoslovakia," Weiss replied.

"To Czechoslovakia?" Moeder looked at him, puzzled. "Where in Czechoslovakia?"

"Theresienstadt," said Weiss. The name sounded unfamiliar.

"Will they send us to another detention camp?" asked another prisoner.

"Well," Mr. Weiss replied and shrugged. "I hope not."

"Maybe it's not true," piped up another prisoner in the group up. "Maybe they'll send us to the gas ovens."

"That's baloney!" shot back Weiss. An apprehensive murmur rose like a cloud of disturbed insects from the undergrowth.

"We have to believe them," Weiss continued quietly. "They didn't need to tell us anything. They simply could have ordered us to board the train and we would be on our way." He shrugged again. "It's as simple as that." He looked around. "So why not believe them?" Nobody answered him.

"I don't trust their words," said the man who before had mentioned the gas ovens. "You can't trust these animals."

"Oh, for God's sake, shut up," snarled another prisoner standing near him.

"Yes," said a nervous voice. "Please, shut your mouth."

The memory of Westerbork and the scraps of paper that were found in returning trains ran through our minds.

There isn't a word to describe our feelings that morning as the soon-to-be passengers milled about the barracks, talking to one another, waiting for the trucks to arrive to the nearby loading platform.

When the first gray trucks came roaring alongside us, sending up sprays of slush, we all fell silent.

It was notable that the SS officers and *Kapos*, who during the last six days had been practically invisible, now suddenly reappeared to oversee a well-ordered departure, but this time without hollering voices or rude expletives. Rather calmly, they directed us toward the spot where we were supposed to board the idling trucks.

Perhaps the reason for this was the close proximity of the now rapidly advancing Allies, which must have scared the heebie-jeebies out of them.

In any event, despite the promising signs of the war imminently coming to a rapid end, there was no excitement among us. Most of us had become emotionally apathetic. Just like the guards, who followed orders, we followed the SS's instructions mechanically.

One by one, the open trucks rolled to a slow stop and lined up single file in front of the first barracks. One SS man directed Moeder, me, and my brothers to the second truck in the convoy. This time there was no name list. We climbed aboard.

A uniformed SS driver sat behind the wheel.

Soon as we started off and headed for the gate, passing the open trailers stacked with bodies, I am sure all of us sitting there in the truck breathed a deep sigh of relief. We were really leaving this squalor, this death-ridden place. As the gates swung open and we turned down the road, I took one last look at the receding camp with its desolate barracks and barbed-wire fence and mentally waved a heartfelt goodbye: *Goodbye, Bergen-Belsen! Goodbye, SS! Goodbye! Goodbye!*

Sitting huddled together with a dozen people in the open truck moving along the rainy winding road, Moeder sat there in silence and stared out at the foggy, wintry flat landscape that streaked past us.

Here and there, lining both sides of the road, were little stucco houses with tile roofs. Staring blankly at the passing gloominess, Ma said bleakly, "I would never have thought that things would end up like this." She shook her head. "Never in my wildest dreams."

I said nothing. What could I say?

I turned to glance at the pine trees and the meadows filled with heather rolling by. Over the sound of the motor, I heard the crackle of small arms fire. Further off was the rumbling of aerial bombardments. For sure the Allied troops were rapidly drawing near now. (We learned later that the Brits entered the camp four days after we left.)

Soon our truck – I counted about a dozen trucks following us on the snaking road – began to pull into a narrow loading platform where a train composed of two-thirds passenger cars and one-third freight cars was waiting. My throat tightened; Lord only knew where that train was taking us.

We pulled to a stop.

The SS drivers climbed down from their cabs and ordered us to dismount. One walked over and dropped our truck's tailgate.

"*Los! Los! Alle raus!*" he ordered crisply. "Everybody out! Out!"

Taking my hand, Moeder turned to me and my brothers. "Let's not lose each other," she urged. "Stay close."

I was feeling pretty shaky and weak as we clambered down from the truck.

Crossing the stony platform, now alive with SS carrying side arms and keeping a watchful eye, we watched a group of men dressed in striped prisoner clothes dismounting from the cars of the waiting train. Who were they? We presumed, hearing them speak German, that they must have been either German deserters or criminals who now would be sent to the camp we had come from. (One section of Belsen had held German deserters.)

As we watched the group disembark, the word spread that they were carriers of a disease and had infected the train.

Actually, at that platform was the first time I heard the words *typhus* and *tuberculosis*, though these epidemics had already been rampant in the camp for weeks due to its poor sanitary conditions.

Lucky me, I thought. I hadn't known. Lucky me.

I followed Moeder across the platform, now packed with people carrying backpacks or dragging suitcases, to one of the empty third-class carriages. I felt sweat dripping from my armpits down the sides of my ribs and experienced a stabbing headache and a dizzy spell that made me stop short in my tracks. Was I running a fever?

SS officers with big pistols in holsters passed by.

People were frantically trying to find pieces of luggage, and the SS were busy directing us to train cars. Before boarding, I caught sight of a scene taking place maybe ten feet from me.

No one seemed to take notice of the group of SS standing in a semi-circle studying a seemingly lifeless male body in prison garb lying on the bloody concrete floor in front of them.

Curious, I stepped forward to get a closer look at the body that was lying there, and I could see through the men that the chest was moving, rose and fell, rose and fell, and the body seemed *alive*, was drawing deep breaths, and as I stared at it, my mouth went dry and a chill shot down my spine.

What had these Nazi savages done to this man?

As I was trying to digest what I was seeing, the SS was standing there casually talking among themselves.

One SS officer said something to Commandant Kramer, who stood there beside him. Then looking around, making sure everybody was watching, he stepped forward and tentatively nudged the body with his booted foot several times. Then stepping back, he threw his head back in uproarious laughter, and the SS surrounding him cheerfully joined in with ribald wicked grins. The SS officer must have said something funny.

Yes, these SS officers were funny people.

"Wolfi?" Moeder was calling me, and I turned and saw her standing nervously in the train doorway. "Come on up, please," she said. She had put the luggage away and glanced across at me.

I walked toward the train.

Where were my brothers? I wondered. I glanced around. They had been directed toward another train car, Moeder told me a little nervously from the train.

People were pushing past me.

When I reached the train compartment, I glanced up at her.

Moeder's eyes searched my face.

"Are you okay?"

I nodded. "Yes, I'm fine."

"Well, come on up, then."

I climbed up the three steps, and we walked into the empty compartment. *Was it real, what I saw? Was it a hallucination?* As I looked out the window and saw the circle of SS officers dispersing and two medics with white armbands easing the corpse onto a stretcher and walking off with it down the length of the platform, I knew that what I had witnessed had been no hallucination but was real, and at that very moment my mind flashed back to that gray wintry morning as my friend Henk's father sat at the table in the barracks and said to us, "Boys, there's not only evil in this world, no, there are also good people, wonderful people out there, plenty, remember boys! There's plenty of wonderful things in this world, remember!" and as I stood there and watched the stretcher and saw a stiffly bent elbow hanging over its side, a dizzying vertigo spell hit me.

My knees went wobbly and the compartment started to spin, round and round and round like a carousel, and sweat started pouring off my brow and began trickling down my back.

I sat down on a wooden bench and leaned back and closed my eyes, and little black spots started dancing in front of my eyes as nausea began to well up. I heard my mother's voice coming from a long way off, and I took a deep breath and then, leaning forward, started vomiting, throwing up everything I had eaten (which had been pitifully little) onto the linoleum floor beneath me. Cold chills started coursing through my body. I found myself trembling and shaking, and the last thing I could remember was German voices outside the window urgently calling out something, like a conductor standing on a railway platform informing passengers to board a train, and then like a movie, everything faded and I passed out.

PART FOUR

The Lost Train

TWENTY-THREE

Circles

The next thing I remember, I was waking up lying on a hardwood bench feeling the bumping wheels of the jouncing train beneath me. Slowly I raised myself up from the battered bench and looked out the window at the war-torn landscape rolling by.

Raindrops streaked across the window. The locomotive gave a loud, piercing whistle.

Moeder sat across from me. She patted me on the knee with a smile on her face. "How are you feeling?"

"Weak."

"Now, you lie back and get some more rest. You must regain your strength."

I nodded. As I lay down, I felt I was floating like a feather, and Moeder sitting opposite me was moving in circles. Her voice was drifting off like a balloon at a funfair, and it seemed like she was speaking in a peculiar sing-song voice, telling me that we were still in Germany, that we had been traveling on the train for over a week now, and the train was traveling and stopping, and whenever it halted, people got off to find something to eat, because no food or drink had been provided.

I was still so tired. My eyes began to close, and suddenly I remembered that I had been throwing up. I leaned slightly over the bench edge to cast a glance at the floor beneath me, but saw no traces, nothing, so

I figured someone must have cleaned it up. Well, I told myself, that's fine with me, and I fell back asleep to the rhythmic sound of the iron wheels clicking across the railroad tracks. I wondered if this was what it felt like to take dope.

At one point, I woke up to the sound of voices coming through the open window. The train had stopped moving. I sat up slowly. A glance around showed me I was alone in the compartment.

I looked out the window and saw maybe thirty feet away a small group of prisoners standing or squatting on their haunches alongside the railroad tracks cooking raw potatoes and green leaves on small fires, and Moeder was there too, sitting on her knees with a scarf wrapped around her dark hair. She was fanning the smoke and flames with a small piece of cardboard.

Very slowly I got up, lowered the window, leaned my head out into the fresh spring air, and saw ahead of me a black locomotive sitting on the railroad tracks hissing white steam and emitting the steady sound of a pounding piston, *boom, boom.*

I closed the window and sat back down.

That day we ate potatoes and green leaves that the prisoners had found in the surrounding fields.

Later, an elderly Dutchman came in and sat down across from me. He was another human skeleton with a shaved skull and hollow eyes in a leathery, wrinkled face. I glanced around the nearly empty car. Two days ago, the car had been crowded. Where had the people gone? I asked the Dutchman about it.

He turned to glance out the window. "Many have died along the way and were buried beside the roadbeds. Many." He turned back to me. "That's why the train cars are slowly getting empty. This disease spreads like wildfire."

He kept on talking. Old timers like to talk. And that was okay with me. I didn't mind. Let him talk. He told me about the week that I had been lying sick on the bench with typhus. It was a miracle that I survived. I was very sick, and he had been sitting right next to Moeder watching her dribble water into my mouth, forcing it down, spoon after spoon, but, he said, I couldn't keep it down and kept throwing up, and she kept trying, over and over.

The old-timer nodded his head slowly, very slowly. Yes, he said, I had been pretty sick, and I was lucky to be alive.

There had been a problem, he continued. I needed to drink lots of fluid, but there was no water, nothing, and when the train stopped, which it did quite often, Moeder and other prisoners got off and collected buckets of water from nearby creeks. There was no way to escape. We were under constant watch by the SS guards. Even though we all knew that liberation was at hand, to the Nazis, orders were orders, and they would follow them to their own end if necessary. So the almost liberated prisoners on this train were to be brought somewhere, and the guards would by God make sure they got there.

As I listened to him, I looked out the window at Moeder sitting there on her knees on the grass under the trees, cooking leaves and potatoes. I asked the man if he knew where we were heading, and he shrugged a very old, tired shrug and said nobody knew, no one.

He reiterated what I had heard previously, that we were heading north to Czechoslovakia. The word was that the train conductor kept searching for rail corridors that had not been bombed yet by the Allied aircraft, and in the meantime the train kept traveling back and forth, back and forth, making frequent stops. Then, he went on, then the SS guards would get off the train to go eat in restaurants in villages nearby, but the prisoners, he told me, knitting his brow, the prisoners got nothing, nada, none, zero, and what they knew for sure was that the Allies kept advancing from all sides, and one day soon the train might get stuck right in the middle, and God only knew what would happen then. And on top of everything, the train had been attacked twice by Allied fighter planes.

"The train has been –?" I stopped and stared at him.

"That's right. Attacked."

I slowly stood as he pointed a bony finger at a wooden side panel, where I saw the bullet holes not only in the train wall but also in the window above it. There was an ugly spider-web crack framing the tableau. *Nice – nice souvenir*, I thought.

I felt a sudden dizziness and quicky sat down.

"Why would the Allies attack us?"

"Why?" Again his old, tired, resigned shrug. "Because the Germans have attached a wagon loaded with heavy weaponry to the back of the train. That's why. We're lucky they only made one pass, then left."

I stared at him and said, "That means the Allies are close."

The old man nodded. "It's only a matter of time now. I hope we can survive until then."

Not long after, the train started moving again.

TWENTY-FOUR

Underway

It was our ninth day on the train, which was hurtling northeast toward the Czech border. Outside, spring seemed near. It had turned sunny again. Occasional clouds drifted slowly across a blue sky. The train lurched and careened. Moeder and the old man were sleeping.

I got up to go to the bathroom. As I moved down the aisle of the train car, my legs quivered and my head spun round and round. The car screeched as the train went around a curve, and I had to steady myself, propping my hands against the aisle seats to stay upright. Slowly, trying hard not to lose my balance, I made my way down the car toward the rear where the toilet was located. My legs shook like leaves, and I felt like I'd just taken a severe bruising in a boxing ring.

As I opened the door and entered the reeking toilet, I found it difficult to breathe. The train toilet lacked a seat. Outside in a corner in the corridor, I had noticed a black-painted iron bucket, which I assumed was put there in case the lavatory was out of order.

Afterwards, I walked shakily like a drunken blind man, holding my arms outstretched, groping my way forward. The train sounded a loud whistle. Flat, brown countryside swept past.

When I got back to my seat, the old-timer was gone. Moeder was still asleep. I stretched out over the two seats opposite her. Three human skeletons sat nearby conversing in soft voices while another prisoner sat slumped on the opposite bench, eyes sunk in his head, dozing.

I closed my eyes and went back to sleep.

I must have slept thirty minutes or so when I was awakened by the sound of a plane passing over us with an ear-deafening roar. Then silence. I sat up and noticed that we had stopped moving again.

The seats around me were empty. Moeder was gone. I turned and looked out the open window at a crowd standing at the edge of a forest. A few in the crowd were hollering something and pointing toward the back of the train. Right then another plane flashed over with a thundering roar.

And then I remembered the old man saying that the Nazis had a wagon filled with weaponry attached to the train.

I watched two white-eyed prisoners getting off the train and running as fast as their legs could carry them toward a nearby pine forest. I was barely able to move but started to get up to exit the train…but too late. Through one of the windows, I saw another plane with the five-pointed star glistening on its wings in the sunlight coming in from the southeast. Whoosh, it flashed over in a thundering boom. And then whoosh, another plane.

I turned and quickly moved back to my seat. Overhead I heard the metallic clatter of machine-gun fire.

Attacking fighter aircraft came in double formation from the southwest and another double from the northeast, flashing over and seconds later roaring back, their nose guns spitting fire at our train. Rounds started whistling through the open window. Down the aisle, a couple of windows exploded. I felt a wave of panic and terror sweep over me and quickly put my head down, closed my eyes tightly and pressed myself as close to the bench as I could get. I lay there motionless, my heart in my throat, afraid to move a muscle. *A wagon loaded with German weaponry attached to the back of our train. Dear God.*

My heart bounced around in my chest, hearing the nerve-racking clatter in the air getting closer and closer. It seemed to go on forever.

And then suddenly, they were gone.

Silence fell. Lying there motionless, I took a deep breath. I wondered where everybody was.

I heard shouts outside. Out the window, I watched prisoners reappearing from the forest. The SS were waving their arms, calling out to the prisoners to get the hell back onto the train.

Multiple explosions had hit the wagon, but the planes were gone for now. Slowly, one after another, the people climbed back onto the train, and then my two brothers and mother were there. My brothers had been in another car with friends from the camp. Moeder's face was filled with worry, and anxiously she asked if I was okay. I told her I was fine. She sat down across from me and explained she had gone to the forest looking for food, and the Germans hadn't allowed anyone to get back on the train once the air raid started.

One hour later, we were traveling again.

Most of the time I slept, but there were scenes, dream-like pictures in my mind that stood out sharply, like a group of pistol-packing SS soldiers standing on a passing station platform with a look of relief that said they were glad the war would soon be over and they could go home, and Moeder seated on the bench urging me to drink and eat whatever she had been able to collect. Sometimes it would be a small potato or a little piece of bread. I believed at one point I was eating a hard-boiled egg; today I wonder whether that had been a fantasy. I have a vague recollection of hearing the Kaddish prayer for the many who died as we traveled.

Slowly I came back to myself, and I became aware that around me were the same hollow-eyed and apathetic sunken faces of near-dead prisoners now trying to outlive the grueling train ride. But in the end, a large number would die of starvation and disease nevertheless.

The weather kept changing; one day was rainy and chilly, then the next was sunshiny and warmer. One early evening, the iron wheels of the train started to screech, and we jolted to another stop. We looked out at a flat pasture with oak trees. There was the smell of spring and fresh cut grass in the air. Far off, we noticed a farming village and could see distant lights of cars moving along a road.

We had pulled up to a gently rising grassy slope.

TWENTY-FIVE

Bread

On what Moeder calculated was something in the neighborhood of the tenth or eleventh day of our journey on the train, we were going through a large forest of pine trees when once again the train stopped. My brothers Eli and Josef, who had come over to our car, were convinced we were in Germany.

It was very quiet. The only noise audible was the hissing locomotive and the pounding of the piston. We sat and speculated how long we would be staying this time. We had gotten accustomed to the frequent stops.

As I looked across the grassy lands to the little distant farmhouses and cars that moved along a country road, I wondered: *Do these people over there live the way I used to live with no fear, where children play and where there's laughter? Do they have enough to eat?*

The steam-hissing and piston-pounding of the locomotive had stopped and suddenly, maybe thirty yards away from us, at the top of the green grassy slope, a middle-aged woman with two small kids appeared, holding a paper bag in her hand.

Soon more women emerged. My brothers guessed that they were locals from the nearby village. They kept a discreet distance from the SS guards, who observed them but didn't say anything. We watched as one of the women took a large piece of bread out of the bag and waved it at us.

Minutes later, the first prisoners emerged from the train and started to scramble their way up to the women, who stood there waiting with the delicious bread in their hands.

I watched them, the survivors, as they grabbed the bread. *Bread. Bread. Bread. Crusty bread. Delicious bread.* My mouth started salivating. I hadn't had food for a lengthy period of time, and the hunger was overwhelming. And I had to regain my strength. Moeder wasn't around, had gone someplace. Outside, I heard loud jabbering as the first prisoners crawled up and then rolled down the grassy slope, fighting each other, trying to get hold of a little piece of bread.

A little voice in the back of my head was saying to me, "Don't just sit there, get up and get something to eat. Go, go, get up," it kept saying, and I got to my feet and shakily descended from the train. I took several steps toward the grassy slope and dodged an inmate who was tumbling down the slope toward the gravel. Then I slowly worked my way up, slowly, very slowly. I crawled on my hands and knees, panting for breath. Soon I began to feel my strength fading away, paused a moment, then doggedly, tenaciously, gritting my teeth grimly, slowly inched my way forward, thinking to myself, *You need the bread, you need the bread, need the bread. Don't stop, keep going*, and I crawled on inch by inch, while a stream of savage curses and eager chattering continued to rage around me. The starving survivors fighting each other for a little crumb of that precious bread seemed like a wild pack of hungry, growling wolves circling a carcass.

I kept spurring myself on, trying hard to pick my way up through the crush to get even an itsy-bitsy crumb of bread. When I finally had almost reached the top, my strength spent, I stopped, took a deep breath, and glanced up with pleading eyes at the three women who were standing there over me.

One of them, staring back down at me with compassionate eyes, was about to toss me a piece of bread when another snarling animal swooped in and triumphantly snatched it away in front of my eyes.

In that moment of despair, I lost my grip and started sliding back down the slope. *Oh, my God no, no.* I slid down, down, but then somehow summoning every ounce of willpower, I managed to dig in my toes and got myself stopped.

I glanced up, breathing hard.

I was maybe ten yards away from the top.

To me, it felt like a hundred.

In disbelief, gathering myself up again, heaving and gasping for breath now, digging in toes and fingernails, clenching my teeth, doggedly I started crawling back up the slope again.

When I finally made it to the top, the three women met my pleading gaze regretfully, shaking their heads, turning their paper bags upside down. Nothing. Nothing. They were empty! Everything was gone!

Tough luck, I told myself. *Tough luck, boy. You just missed it, okay?*

The women took their children and began the walk back to the village. Shaking my head, trying to still my quivering legs, I stared vacantly after them. Pausing another moment to get my breath back, I turned and started to slide down the slope toward the railroad tracks and back aboard the train.

A little later, the locomotive sounded a short whistle blast, the train gave a jerk, and we were traveling again.

All that night and the following morning, the train continued. My mother was certain we were traveling through East Germany, though how she could guess this from the flattened towns and shell-smashed buildings, I'll never know.

On the third day of that week, the train reached a deserted suburb of Berlin.

The German sky was a bright, cloudless blue. The train had stopped again. (This moving back and forth of the train had become an endless broken record.)

This time, we stopped at a small, roofed-over open-air railway station in what looked like a large city. A broken sign in the station read "BERLIN-FRIEDRICHSHAIN." All around us, as far as the eye could see, not a single building had been left standing. Only rubble.

We opened the window and looked out. The air was cool and crisp. We saw rubble and ruins everywhere, a ghastly skeleton of a once large, elegant city.

There was an eerie silence, and not a soul was to be seen.

The only sound we heard was the hissing and pounding of the locomotive. We sat down and waited. Through the broken windows, we saw a couple of SS guards standing on the platform. The train guards joined them. It looked like they were getting a report about what had happened.

We couldn't hear what they were saying and just sat there for a long five minutes, listening to the unsettling hissing of the locomotive.

Then suddenly a piercing siren cut the air with a shrieking, nerve-racking undulating wail. Over and over and over. It seemed as though the siren wouldn't stop. We gazed at each other and looked out the window. What was going on? Nothing moved. Nothing stirred.

Two SS guards, rifles slung over their shoulders, hurried past our window along the platform, waving their arms frantically, hollering to the train driver to get the hell out of the station.

"*Raus! Raus!*" they shouted, "*Los! Los!* Quick! Out!"

I got up from the bench, leaned my head out the open window, and saw two – no, three – SS soldiers swinging up onto the moving train, waving their arms, yelling, "*Los, raus! Raus!* Come on, out! Out!"

Farther off, another air-raid siren was dying down.

The train let out a long whistle. I pulled my head back inside. Must be another air raid, I thought.

I sat down. We watched the shot-up buildings slide by as the train, slowly swaying, started to pull out. Seeing all around us the entire city flattened, we wondered what the planes were going to attack, since there was nothing left to attack but ghostly remains.

Impatiently, I stood up again, despite Moeder admonishing me to sit back down, and looked out the open window. Suddenly, though we had not heard any planes, as I turned my head I could see the black stick of bombs tumbling down from the sky onto the railroad station, as though they had materialized out of the ozone.

Seconds later, there was an earth-shaking explosion, and a giant fireball shot up in the air. The railroad station went up in dancing flames and smoke, and a geyser of debris spouted into the air, followed by multiple explosions. The small railroad station we had just left was within seconds ablaze with a furious roaring fire.

Moeder and other prisoners who stood beside me now stepped back. We closed the window and sat down, silent. The train let out another long whistle and sped up.

Looking outside, we thanked our lucky stars we were still alive and unharmed.

Lucky for us, the SS was warned just in time. *Lucky, lucky.*

TWENTY-SIX

The Cossack

Liberation came for us on the twelfth day of the train journey. Railways had been destroyed, and trains were bombed. The SS guards had been trying to find passages to get through.

And now we came to a halt in the countryside on the German-Polish border. I remember the date: April 23, 1945. We stopped in a small German village called Tröbitz.

I can remember that morning. Dawn was coming up in the east. The smells of ripe fields and pines filled the air. Somewhere in the distance were rumbling explosions. And then silence. Then the rattle of small-arms fire went off. Again silence.

Suddenly, something unexpected happened.

Looking out the train compartment's window, we saw the SS guards, hands raised above their heads, being marched off at gunpoint by khaki-uniformed soldiers.

Moeder turned to me in astonishment. "What is happening here?"

We were getting off the train to find out what was going on when I stopped short and pointed a finger to an olive-drab uniformed soldier sitting on a horse at the edge of a pine forest. He wore a black Cossack fur hat, his machine gun lay across his saddle, and his brown leather boots were stuck in metal stirrups. He glanced at us for a moment and then led his horse at a slow trot in our direction.

He stopped in front of us, gave a frowning look, and asked, "*Kto ky?*" (Who are you?).

Moeder, knowing some Russian (she had spent the early part of her childhood in Poland), glanced at him and then looked back at me. "He's a Russian officer," she told me. "He speaks Russian."

"*Nemetskiy?*" (German?), the soldier asked, looking from his horse down at us, knitting his brow suspiciously.

Moeder shook her head quickly. "No, no, we are Dutch. Holland. The Netherlands."

"Aha!" He nodded. "*Gollandia, da, da.*"

He turned to stare at the group of human skeletons that had started to gather around us. Then from the train more human skeletons began to emerge. The Russian officer glanced toward them, then back at us, and then without a word wheeled his horse, said something like, "*Idti!*" spurred it and galloped away toward the pine forest.

"It's over," someone said. "The Germans are gone."

"The Russians," added someone else, "have come to liberate us."

That was our first taste of freedom.

And so we were liberated.

The SS guards had been marched off at gunpoint by Russian military men. With the Cossack's appearance, we suddenly realized we were free. Such a blasé ending to two and a half years living through the horrors of the camps.

Most camp survivors remained calm, too sick to stand or move and too apathetic to even celebrate their newfound freedom. I was still too dazed from my illness to think straight. Later on we would think a great deal about losing our father, about the friends we knew who had been left behind in the camp, and of course, all those who had died such pointless and horrible deaths.

Not long after that, things started to move fast.

The Russian military set up a command office in the nearby village of Tröbitz and moved the survivors into houses of German civilians, some of whom had fled the advancing Russian forces.

Moeder, my two brothers, and I came to live in a three-bedroom house with Klara Bertram, a stout-looking housewife in her forties, and her redheaded eighteen-year-old daughter Margit. Klara's husband had been killed on the Eastern Front.

We learned from them that Tröbitz was a village of about seven hundred people.

One morning over a cup of coffee, housewife Klara admitted to Moeder that people of the village believed that Jews were monstrous creatures with horns on their heads, although they had never seen any Jewish people in their entire lives.

Our prime concern after the liberation was food. We were dehydrated itinerants wandering the desert looking for water. And there was never enough food.

Due to the long, extensive period of warfare, the Germans themselves had a critical shortage of food. Margit, the red-haired eighteen-year-old daughter, explained to us (my brothers and I had picked up a smattering of German at home and in the camp), that the German transportation system had been systematically bombed by the Allies, which had severely hampered the food supply.

The two women shared whatever edible things were available, which was often canned meat that they had kept stocked in the basement or home-made bread. Sometimes there was soup, and there were fruits and vegetables growing in the little garden in front of the small house.

My family and I, like all other people in the camp, had lost a great deal of weight. Garments that the locals collected for the camp survivors simply fell off us.

It felt good to be back in the free world, though the first days were weird, really. We had a hard time adapting to looking out the window and not hearing the screaming SS and seeing no barbed-wire fence surrounding us.

About two weeks after we got liberated, my oldest brother Eli came down with typhus. I remember seeing his face flushed with fever, and he kept complaining of persistent abdominal pain. Moeder, who some-times alternated with the young woman Margit, sat at his bedside as his young body was fighting the disease that night. Fortunately it was a mild case of the disease. It took him about ten days – after a house call from a doctor, taking some home remedies, and drinking lots of liquids – to slowly get back on his feet.

One pleasant mid-morning, I stepped out the door of the house and walked down the main street, passing rows of gray-painted brick homes with well-maintained gardens. As I walked along the street, I stopped to watch a stocky Russian soldier dressed in Russian uniform roping a little pig to a thick tree trunk.

What would he do that for? I thought. Around me, passersby stopped to stare at him.

One bystander, a fellow survivor who spoke Russian, told us the soldier took pity on the survivors and wanted to give them something good to eat.

After having tied the pig to the tree, the soldier took a couple of steps back, removed the service revolver from his holster, leveled it at the animal, and fired two short bursts. The pig gave a high-pitched squeal, went down on its knees, thrashed about wildly for a long min-ute, and then went over on its side and lay still.

We passersby stood there and gaped at it.

After shooting the animal, the soldier calmly holstered his pistol and without a word to us, turned and walked away. Maybe half a dozen of the survivors stood there perplexed for a moment and then went to their houses and fetched big kitchen knives. They then cut large slices of meat from the animal and brought it back home and cooked it. That was the first taste of a great meal we survivors had savored in a very long time. After the concentration camps, you'll eat what you can get.

However, not all was fine. Not by a long shot.

When night fell in Tröbitz, things got nasty. Drunk Russian sol-diers would go from door to door wherever Germans lived. Without knocking, they forced their way inside and looked for women. It had become a nightly routine for them, and when it was getting dark, German women – young and old – were scared out of their wits.

And then the wrist watches! Goodness. They wanted them like small children wanted toys and would mercilessly pilfer watches wherever they could find them. With drawn guns.

We figured that sooner or later, we would have to leave here. But for the time being, we were content to live in this peaceful pleasant village with its old houses, green lawns, and surrounding woodlands.

It had been almost a month. The typhus epidemic continued raging, and many people became ill. Maybe that was the reason, I figured, not too many people were seen out on the streets, except for Soviet soldiers who sometimes would march in long columns, five abreast, singing Russian songs while female soldiers would join in with brilliant soprano voices.

Sitting with my feet curled up on a stone wall, I would watch this spectacle as they marched down the streets. Sometimes there was a Russian dance performance in the main square in front of the major's rose-brick office building. Villagers would sit on stone benches under rows of shaded elm trees in front of the building and watch female Russian soldiers pertly swinging their hips, dancing round and round and round, singing and clapping hands in a fast rhythm as other soldiers played the balalaika. Then two Soviet male soldiers would squat down, cross their arms, and kick their legs out in a fast tempo as the rest of them stood in a circle playing the accordion and fifes while beating time with their feet.

TWENTY-SEVEN

Pause

As the days wore on in Tröbitz, and the two German women we lived with found themselves slowly running out of food, I decided to go to nearby villages to try to get food there. I didn't know if the people living there would have more food, but I figured it was worth a try.

About one month after the grueling train ride, I had gained strength and was confident I would be able to walk the distance without much trouble. After breakfast I told Moeder and my two brothers what I planned to do. Joop (that's what we sometimes called Josef in Holland) stared at me. "You want to go to the villages and ask people for food?"

I nodded yes.

Eli, my oldest brother, smiled. "Good idea," he said. "I wish you good luck." He frowned a moment. "It's a long walk."

"Not that long," I said. "Margit told me it's about thirty minutes."

Joop was thoughtful. "You sure you want to go there?"

"Sure." I shrugged. "No problem, I feel fine. I can walk that far."

Eli gave me another smile and slapped me on the back. "Hats off to you," he said. He had recovered from typhus, and both my brothers told me they would have liked to come along but had already arranged to meet with friends from the camp in town.

I nodded. "It's okay," I said. "I'll manage."

Walking outside in the streets, I recognized a few of the sick camp survivors who apparently had recovered, looking almost human again.

The nearest village to Tröbitz was Schilda, about four kilometers away.

So on that sunny May morning, I set out for the village.

Moeder hadn't been feeling too well. She told me she would rest a while and wait till I got back.

It was a pleasant walk in the morning sun alongside the winding road with the smell of asphalt and with the green pine forests and the brighter green of the flatlands surrounding me. Here and there, a bicycle rider or an automobile was driving by.

As I walked the two and a quarter miles (3.5 km) at a steady pace, a slight summer breeze was blowing.

Soon, ahead, I saw the first lovely white single-family homes nestled under a grove of old trees. It looked like a fairytale setting. All around me was deep silence. Here and there, birds were chirping in the trees or a dog was barking in the distance.

A hint of cattle manure scent lingered in the air.

I was heading south when I came to a one-story house surrounded by elm trees. The forest-green shades were pulled down over the windows, and I wondered whether anyone was living inside or whether they had fled the advancing Red Army. Klara, the housewife we were staying with, had told us that a vast number of Germans had fled the Soviet army.

I gathered my courage and knocked on the front door of the stone house. Maybe a caring person would come out and invite me in and serve me all kinds of yummy food?

But nothing happened. Nothing moved. I waited a bit longer. The door didn't open. Okay. I moved toward another identical house, next door, a gray single-family home with a sloping roof. I knocked on the door and waited. Same result.

I turned and walked over to the next home, a white-plastered two-story farmhouse with an adjacent old stone barn. I knocked three times on the brown painted door. *Knock, knock, knock.* Tomblike silence. A strong smell of summer and fresh-cut hay swirled through the air. I waited. Crows were cawing nearby. Seconds passed. Then the front door was stealthily opened, and an elderly woman peered out at me, but she quickly closed the door. Terrific. But it didn't discourage me. On the contrary, stubbornly I kept knocking on three more doors. People in the fourth home were more forthcoming. The place was a nice yellow brick farmhouse shaded by two old willowy oaks and was set apart from the other houses.

I knocked two times. After a moment, a slight young woman with a friendly face stood inside the doorway with two small girls and stared at me.

I said, "*Guten Tag.*"

She nodded her head. "*Guten Tag.*"

After she listened to my wishes, she gave a knowing nod. She must have realized that I was one of the camp survivors who had landed in Tröbitz.

"Wait here," she said to me. "I'll be right back."

She hurried back inside with the kids and came back out a few moments later with two shopping bags. She showed me what goodies she had put into the bags, reached into one of them and pulled out some bread rolls, a tin of condensed milk, homemade jam, and some apples and pears (which must have grown in her garden). I stood gaping. Some of it she had put in a blue insulator box. Handing the bags to me, she pointed a finger at it and asked, "Will you be able to carry all this back to the village?"

I nodded yes.

"Good." She smiled warmly, held out her hand, and wished me good luck.

I shook it, and I thanked her.

Then the mother with her children stepped back and slowly closed the door.

I stood there and looked down at myself and thought, you are looking like some fearsome scarecrow, Wolf. Though in much better shape than before, I still was all bones and skin. Anyway, the warmth and kind-heartedness of this family had been wonderfully invigorating.

On the way back, I had to rest several times. Once I sat down on the grass under a grove of trees near the edge of a dense wood that gave way to fields of hay, and I watched as the cars drove past.

A bicycle rider, a big man in his sixties with a dour expression, stopped by. He made his way across the field toward me, got off his bike, let it drop to the ground, and sat down across from me and began to speak to me in German.

I had picked up enough German in the Nazi camp to understand him.

He must also have realized just by my looks that I was one of those survivors who had wound up in the village of Tröbitz.

At one point during our brief conversation, he eyed the two bags with food I had set down beside me, got up, took a peek into one, pointed a beefy finger at it, then sitting back down asked if I would trade the food for his old bicycle. I could tell that he was baiting me.

Sitting there, I listened quietly as he spoke. When he finished, I looked at him and said in broken German, "*Sie wollen tauschen altes Fahrrad für gutes Essen?*" (You want me to trade old bicycle for good food?). I shook my head. "You are kidding, right? All this delicious food for that ridiculous bicycle you've got there?" I stared at him and asked, "Are you serious?"

He nodded his big head. "*Jawohl.*"

Again I shook my head disbelievingly. That food was not worth trading for anything in the world, not even gold. I looked at him and said, "You must be out of your mind."

He studied me for a long moment with narrowed eyes and then got up.

"You know what?" he scowled at me.

I glanced up at him. "What?"

He shot me a hard look and snarled viciously, "You are a *real* little Jew, aren't you?"

Muttering under his breath, "Money-grabbing kikes!" he bent down to pick up his bike by the handlebars, straightened, turned back to me and shouted, "Damn you! Damn you! All of you!" Then he jumped on his bike and, still cursing me with a continuous stream of invective, started to pedal furiously away across the grass toward the asphalt road.

I got to my feet and looked after him. A torrent of emotions surged through me. This German had the gall to talk to me like that, so soon after what had happened to us? I watched him pedaling down the road until he disappeared from sight. I wanted to do something, anything, but what could I do against that big German ox?

For a brief moment I saw myself hollering and throwing rocks after him (there were plenty of stones lying around in the grassy field to pick up and hurl after him), but what was the point? What did I expect? It wouldn't do any good.

Across from me, a light breeze was moving the branches and leaves in the treetops.

I picked up the shopping bags from the grass and started up the road to Tröbitz.

It seemed like a longer walk this time, and I had to sit down three times and rest. I was drenched in sweat and wrung out when I arrived back at the house, where I received a joyous reception from Moeder and from Frau Klara Bertram and her daughter Margit.

Grabbing the paper sacks and emptying them on the old table, they gaped with wide eyes as the tin of condensed milk, the bread rolls, fruit, and the rest of the food rolled out. Moeder clapped her hands together and then gave me a proud hug. Both Klara and Margit joined in.

I remember I wanted to eat and eat, and even after I was full, I still would keep on eating.

This feeling, this craving for food, accompanied me for many years to come.

TWENTY-EIGHT

Underway Again

It was June, and we were still in Tröbitz. A sense of restless impatience had been hanging in the air, and we kept wondering what was going to happen to us. How much longer were we going to have to wait in this quiet village? Waiting for what? To go home? Where was home? Where would we be going? The Russians didn't have any information about the future. While we were grateful for being safe and free, it was frustrating not knowing what our future held.

On a sunny day in early June, Moeder was overtaken with a serious illness. There were rose-colored spots appearing on her face and arms, and she started to cough and complained of severe headaches. She couldn't get out of bed, she was so weak.

One look at her told me what was wrong. I swallowed hard. I had experienced this awful disease and had seen the suffering all around me. The following day she was delirious, murmured incoherently, and ran a fever of 104 (40 degrees Celsius).

When the doctor came and examined her, he told us bluntly, "Your mother has typhus. She needs to be admitted to the hospital." On his way to the door, he stopped a moment. "I'll see to it that she will be taken care of right away," he said, and left the room.

One hour later, a bright green ambulance with a red cross on its side arrived at the house, and Moeder was taken to a hospital in Tröbitz

Nordfeld, a few miles away. I stood outside in the street, watching the ambulance turn the corner, and felt a lump in my throat. I hoped she'd be all right. Over the next weeks, my brothers and I tried several times to visit her, but the doctors at the hospital wouldn't allow anybody in, to prevent the spread of the epidemic.

After the ambulance left, I noticed people standing in front of a neighbor's house, talking and gesturing excitedly. I stopped to watch as more people came out to the street. Quite a few stopped to listen and then started up the street.

What's going on? I wondered, and my brothers and I followed the crowd as they were making their way toward the village's main square. Once there, we saw a young American soldier in khaki uniform, web belt and pistol slung cowboy style low on the hips, one hand resting on his holster flap, standing in an open-top jeep in the middle of the crowd. We pushed our way through to listen to what he had to say. Of course, he spoke in English, and we couldn't understand any of it. Luckily, there was a Dutch woman who could speak English fluently who was listening intently, even asking him questions.

After several minutes of talking, the crowd stepped back to make room as the soldier climbed down from the jeep and made his way toward the Russian commandant's pastel-colored office building. We stood there in a circle listening to the young woman who had asked the questions, translating into Dutch what she had learned.

It turned out that a couple of days earlier, two survivors of the camp had left Tröbitz on bicycles, and on the way back to Holland informed the Americans stationed in Delitzsch (a small town in eastern Germany) about us, and now the American liaison officer had been sent to Tröbitz on specific orders of the US Third Army Command in Leipzig to discuss with Russian military authorities repatriation of survivors in Tröbitz to their countries.

Hearing this, the crowd broke into cheerful applause.

We had been living in the village for over seven long weeks. Now things began to accelerate like an express train.

We were instructed to make preparations for transport to Leipzig, in northeastern Germany. We would travel by trucks. The sick would make the trip in ambulances. Moeder, the hospital had notified us, would be among them. One week later, a convoy of US military trucks arrived in the square in the center of the village.

Housewives and kids had moved out into the street to say goodbye to us. Shopkeepers had filled the sidewalks and wished us good luck.

I saw my two brothers advancing slowly in a long line, ahead of me. The first in line began to climb into the first truck.

I was waiting in front of the long row of US Army trucks when a white and red Russian ambulance pulled up in the middle of the *Dorfplatz*. I watched as Russian paramedics in olive green uniforms opened the back doors and started moving patients on stretchers toward the waiting American ambulances.

Noticing four female Russian stretcher bearers approaching the American ambulance, I spotted Moeder lying on the gurney, covered by a pastel blue blanket. I walked over and told them that I wanted to speak to her. I remembered the word in Russian for mother and said, "*Mamushka.*"

I stared at Moeder in shocked silence. *Goodness*, I thought, feeling my heart plunge within me. I hardly recognized her.

Her eyes had sunk deep into her head, and her cheekbones jutted out alarmingly. She appeared more emaciated – if that were possible – than when I last had seen her.

"Mama?" I murmured.

She glanced up at me, barely able to talk. "Are you all right?"

I nodded my head, silent.

Passersby stopped and watched.

The four attendants from the ambulance stood waiting.

From a radio somewhere, a German song carried faintly across the square, drifting through the balmy summer air to us.

Doors of other ambulances clanged shut. There was a rapid exchange in Russian, and the Soviet nurses started to move. I walked alongside the gurney until we had reached the American ambulance.

A US paramedic stood there waiting and opened the back doors.

The Russians carrying the gurney paused a moment. Moeder glanced across at me and said, "Take good care of yourself, Wolfi." Her voice cracked. "You hear?" There were tears in her eyes.

I nodded my head and watched as the medics slid the gurney with Moeder into the rear of the ambulance. I watched as the doors were closing and felt my stomach twist into a knot. *Will I ever see Moeder again?* Moments later, the engine sprang to life, and the ambulance drove away.

I picked up the few belongings I had accumulated in Tröbitz and started toward the column of trucks where a group of GIs was waiting. One of the soldiers, standing by the second truck with a list in his hand, checked off our names, and my brothers and I climbed into one of the open military trucks.

As I sat there, I watched a German local speaking to a GI who was lighting up a cigarette. The German held out a hand and the US soldier ignored him, looked away, and kept smoking his cigarette.

It was general knowledge in those days that the US military discouraged fraternizing between GIs and German civilians.

A few minutes later, we started off.

The distance to Leipzig was about fifty-five miles (90 km).

The drive would last about an hour and forty minutes.

PART FIVE

Will We Ever Get Home?

TWENTY-NINE

The American

We were traveling across the German autobahnen at a good pace. There was a refreshing northern wind blowing in our faces. We passed fields of grain and barley and here and there little villages with two- and three-house hamlets and cattle grazing beneath the tall trees in the sun.

Reaching Leipzig, we were put up in a former German army barracks in the center of town, a drab two-story building with green painted walls and polished concrete floors. Being housed in a former SS barracks, naturally, triggered bad memories.

The days in Leipzig passed swiftly. All around us in the streets, we saw American soldiers walking around the rubble-filled streets, snapping photos and enjoying the bars and cafes when they weren't on duty.

Our barracks was located near a US military base, and at daybreak, we would hear a noncom's hoarse voice coming through the open windows counting a steady cadence: "Left, right, left, right, get in step, left…left…"

The first morning we heard this, my brothers and I got up to look out the window and watched columns of uniformed GIs marching in formation across the asphalt road under rows of elms, singing drill songs.

This sight of someone else having to show up early in the morning while we slept in late finally penetrated the fog I was in, and I knew

147

the feeling of true freedom. After the camp, it was like another world, another universe.

The days in Leipzig passed swiftly.

I spent part of the time going to the United Nations Relief and Rehabilitation Administration (UNRRA) office inquiring about Moeder's whereabouts and condition. Officials in charge had no information about her location, neither what city she was in nor what hospital she had been taken to.

There was a café-bar named Arkada – a favorite of US servicemen – located not far from our barracks. The bar was usually crowded and smoky inside, and there was loud laughter as an old radio played German music and American pop songs. GIs would sit at little wooden tables, some playing cards, some chatting away while drinking cups of coffee or having rounds of beer or wine. My brothers, being older, loved to go there. The café supplied soft drinks and mineral water bottles to our barracks, and I often went there to pick them up.

One day, as I walked in, I noticed three uniformed GIs sitting at a corner table. I observed them for a while. They were laughing as they drank the German wine and talked about whatever GIs talked about. The men were obviously having a good time. One of the three men seated at the table, a lanky, long-jawed uniformed soldier in his twenties, glanced at my frail figure, said something to his two companions, stood up and made his way to me.

"Do you speak English?"

My eyes narrowed. "Dutch."

He smiled at me. "I understand Dutch."

We shook hands. He told me that his name was Pete Hoekstra, and I introduced myself.

He invited me to come over to their table to meet his buddies.

As we started toward their table, Hoekstra gave me a curious sideways glance, and said, "I heard that you were in one of those Nazi concentration camps."

I nodded my head. It must have been obvious I had been in the camp, and I'm sure he didn't have to hear about it. One look at me would tell him.

When we reached the table, he indicated a chair. "Have a seat."

He introduced me to his friends, ordered a beer for himself and his two buddies and a soft drink for me, and soon they began to ask questions about the camp. I told them all they wanted to know about what we'd gone through as prisoners of the Nazis. When I described the hours-long roll calls during the freezing winters and piles of bodies carried on trolleys to the crematorium, the GIs' brows furrowed. They seemed angry.

For a while, I kept seeing Pete Hoekstra in that coffee bar.

One day, as we were seated at the corner table in the crowded room, Hoekstra put down his glass – a sign that he was about to say something important. As was our custom, he spoke to me in Dutch, then translated my answers to his comrades in English. "If your mother doesn't come back, maybe you'd like to move to America?"

I stared back at him. "How do you mean?"

He was aware of my status, that my father had died and so far there was no word of my mother, and he told me if things, God forbid, turned out bad for me, his family would be willing to act as a sponsor and adopt me.

But all I could manage to say at that moment was, "Adopt me?"

He smiled. My surprise must have been obvious.

"Yes, they are living in California," he said. "In Long Beach." He spread his arms wide. "The US is a great place. Lots of opportunities." He nodded. "They are nice people, real down to earth." He paused. "Well?"

I thought for a moment. "What about my two brothers?" I asked. My brothers had several times stopped at the Arkada Café, and he had greeted them. He paused a moment. "There are quite a few families," he said, "like my family, who want to adopt children who managed to survive the camps. We might," he added with a smile.

I studied his face. "Are you serious?"

He nodded again. "Of course."

Me, move to America? Move with this serviceman I had not previously known to the United States?

There had been some talk about orphans surviving the Nazi camps who found new homes in the US and had been adopted by GIs stationed in Germany. For a brief moment, it was an exciting thought; suddenly a new future seemed to open up before me. Trying to digest what I had been hearing, I asked myself if I could believe it. I didn't know, and anyway there was, of course, Moeder. I had no idea where she was, didn't know about her condition, didn't know how she was doing. And then there were my two brothers, and anyhow, it seemed to me all idle talk, nothing serious, really – and I was right.

As a big influx of GIs poured in from other army bases across West Germany, I lost sight of Hoekstra and assumed that he might have gotten reassigned to another outfit or had been shipped home.

Although the notion of my being adopted and living in America was squelched, I was feeling upbeat; there were still people who were ready to help. After all I had been through, to have him smile warmly and pat me on the shoulder and tell me he wanted to help showed me he cared. It was a gesture of comfort and of hope. It was America to me.

Meanwhile the group of Dutch survivors who had survived the train journey and lived in Tröbitz were informed that we would leave for Holland two weeks earlier than scheduled.

THIRTY

Back in Holland

On Sunday, July 29, 1945, the Bergen-Belsen camp survivors were seated in comfortable compartments of a special passenger train (organized by UNRRA) bound for Maastricht, South Holland, about 130 miles (212 km) from home. The travel time, including the various station stops in Germany, was eight hours.

Memories of the time we spent on that train remain with me today.

There was a wonderful smell of delicious food hovering in the air.

During the trip, US servicemen were serving us hot coffee and slices of crispy snow-white vegetarian sandwiches that tasted like heaven.

Their shirt sleeves rolled up above their elbows, they would walk up and down the train aisle, carrying loaded trays, and with warm smiles on their faces would call out, "More coffee? More sandwiches?"

It seemed unreal, like a mirage.

There had been several train stops at German railroad stations. One stop was at Erfurt, 185 miles (300 km) west of Berlin.

When the train stopped, we got up and looked out the open window at a long, roofed-over platform.

There was a roaring noise of trains pulling in and out of the station. The constant sound of metallic German voices was heard over loudspeakers, and as far as our eyes could see, there was a mass of German people standing there, elderly people and young children with mothers. We guessed that many Germans were homeless after their houses had been bombed. Others were scared to death and were fleeing westward from the rapidly advancing Red Army that was about to take over the eastern zone of Germany. Some of them were standing or sitting on backpacks or wooden crates beside the railroad track, glancing at our stationary train with vacant eyes.

I watched them from the train window. Now they were the ones on the run.

At one point, as I was about to go to the rear of the train to get some refreshments, a US serviceman standing right behind me was leaning forward to get a closer look at the crowd waiting there on the long platform. Turning toward me, his eyes searching my face curiously, his expression seemed to say, *What do you think about these poor things standing out there on the platform?* The truth was, these Germans left me completely cold. I couldn't have cared less.

Half an hour later, we started off and arrived early in the evening in the city of Maastricht, where we were housed in a long, gloomy high-ceilinged hall of a former elementary school with windows on both sides and rows of makeshift beds lining the bare inside walls.

A couple of days after our arrival, UNRRA officials began to repatriate us to our different hometowns. Finally it was homecoming, and we were back in Amsterdam, the city where it all had started. We were quartered in a former Jewish hospital for seniors called the Joodse Invalide, located in the center of Amsterdam. In the postwar period, the six-story building had served as an asylum and provided aid to a large group of homeless Jews and Gentiles.

Our house was no longer ours, and we had to live in this former hospital that had been transformed into a home for refugees. I was assigned to a separate dormitory room from my brothers, with boys more or less my age on the second floor – the orphans' floor. For the first time in a long time, I was living an ordinary life in a well-kept building, sleeping in my own bed, and sitting at a properly set table and eating as much as I wanted, a glorious feeling!

And now, the feeling of *liberation* we all had repressed for such a long time flooded over all of us.

The word had some kind of surreal connotation.

We had lived like on another planet; now, people around us seemed to move about light-heartedly without really seeming to have to carry the albatross of a grievous past.

We felt reborn and wanted to adapt to this new free life quickly.

But it took time.

Many of us had recurring nightmares and woke up in the middle of the night reliving the fiendish memories of the Nazi concentration camps.

Survivors hoped to wriggle out of it. Some of us did, others didn't. A few went crazy, and some committed suicide.

The truth was nobody came back without scars.

We still had no information about Moeder's condition. Was she alive? Did she survive the illness? Had she died? What was her condition?

Meanwhile, like people almost dying of thirst getting their canteen filled, we started to relish life to its fullest. We definitely did; we savored, indulged, and reveled in our newly regained *freedom*.

We had a lot of catching up to do, and boy, we sure did. When night fell, we went out with Jewish and non-Jewish girls at the Joodse Invalide to the roaring carnival, the *kermis*, on the outskirts of town. To us who had lived in filthy barracks behind electrified fences, who had gotten used to piles of corpses and never knew which one of us would die that day, this carnival was like opening the door to another universe.

We gaped wide-eyed in rapt, disbelieving fascination at the breathtaking thrill rides and dazzling glittering lights and listened in speechless awe to the cheery laughter of the crowd that swirled around us and to the tinkling tinny music of the merry-go-rounds and the hollering voices of pitchmen who welcomed us to their booths. With pounding hearts, we rode the whooshing, shrieking roller coasters and simply took delight in our newly regained lifestyle.

Those of us youngsters who had been in camps enrolled in a temporary school to catch up on what we had missed. Some of us, including me, took up boxing classes (skipping rope, learning how to move, guard, punch, and defend), with the intention of never being humiliated again should we face tough ruffians in dark alleyways.

But first and foremost, we wanted to forget the ghosts of the past, to enjoy life. We sure rejoiced, but there was something, something indefinable, something that seemed to cling to us like a burr – you know, when you toss it, it keeps sticking to your jacket. Surely you want to know what it is? Fine, listen closely, here it is: we were filled with a wild, savage hatred, hated everything German with a cold, fierce hostility, loathed whatever was Nazi-related. Everything that was clearly discernibly German we considered evil; they were the despised foe, and we solemnly promised to wreak vengeance upon them until the last murdered victim had been avenged.

Some might invoke the hallowed words of the wise men saying something about how we shall forgive and therefore be blessed, because forgiveness is the redemption of the soul. Fine. Great. But there are other words, from the Torah, burned into our memory. Again, listen carefully, here it is:

> Remember what the Amalekites did to you along the way when you came out of Egypt. When you were weary and worn out, they met you on your journey and attacked all who were lagging behind; they had no fear of God. When the Lord your God gives you rest from all the enemies around you in the land he is giving you to possess as an inheritance, you shall blot out the name of Amalek from under heaven. Do not forget! (Deuteronomy 25:17–19)

We shall abhor the tormentor with every fiber of our being and *not* forget and *not* forgive. We will remember our enemy till the very end, because *remembrance* is of the essence here – and that's what we camp survivors, after our liberation, had been thinking…

THIRTY-ONE

A Miracle

Amsterdam, May 1946.

It was a miracle.

The authorities told us when she would be coming in by plane to Amsterdam from Kaiserslautern, Germany, where she had been recuperating for over a year. My brothers and I were ecstatic.

I remember that it was a spring-like day, sunny with a deep blue sky. Eli and Josef went with me to Schiphol Airport, about five and a half miles (9 km) southwest of Amsterdam.

We stood there in the crowded hall and waited impatiently for the first passengers to deplane. Mama saw us, hesitated, and then smiled and waved. She was dressed in a light gray coat over a beige suit. She still looked somewhat frail, but she was alive and well. We rushed toward her, hugged, and exclaimed with huge smiles, "Welcome back to the free world, Mama."

It was over.

Epilogue

World War II ended in Europe officially on May 8, 1945. Over fifty million people had been killed, and six million Jews out of 9.5 million who lived in Europe before the war had been murdered. The continent was left a shambles; it was chaos and despair. Licking its wounds, the population of the European countries was trying to find the way back to normalcy.

Return to normalcy; what did that mean? I didn't know at the time. At thirteen and a half years old, I was a survivor of the concentration camps of Westerbork and Bergen-Belsen. By the time my brothers Eli and Joseph and I returned to Amsterdam, four months had passed since our liberation.

We were living in a former hospital building right in the center of Amsterdam under the supervision of a family who were also refugees from Bergen-Belsen.

A temporary Jewish school for refugees was established soon, and I found myself sitting in a classroom of survivors of various ages, none of whom were particularly interested in what was being taught. That was okay, because the school was short on school supplies. I remember and was told by survivor friends that I was very rebellious and angry during this time; sometimes we survivor boys had fights with Dutch youngsters, particularly when antisemitic insults were thrown at us.

My brothers Eli, seventeen, and Josef, sixteen, went to a different school and were occupied with themselves. I was pretty much on my own, doing practically whatever came to my mind. And a new daily routine started for me.

The mornings I spent at school, and the long afternoons I had for myself. It didn't take long for me and other youngsters who lived in the same building to band together and form a gang to steal things that would sell quickly, enabling us to go to the movies, to swimming pools, whatever. We didn't care much for morals or rules, as long as we had a real good time, great fun, and a good laugh. That was my new kind of normalcy – living without any responsibility and accountability and feeling free as a bird. We did not really care about anything during that time.

Interestingly, during this period, none of us spoke about our experiences in the camps. We wanted to forget the past. But the hatred we had for those who had caused all that misery didn't diminish one iota. We youngsters expressed loudly our deep aversion and promised ourselves never to forget or forgive the Germans and Germany. When, years later, I learned about the capture of Adolf Eichmann, the chief executioner of the "Final Solution," the systematic genocide of European Jewry, I experienced a deep sense of satisfaction.

I had closely followed the Nuremberg trials after the war. There were quite a number of SS, mostly the high brass, who were indicted for war crimes and sentenced to death by hanging. But where were the others, all the low-ranking SS henchmen? Like that brutal sadist the SS guard Pavlenko who'd beaten Moeder – where was he? Did he escape? Was he hiding out somewhere, living the good life someplace and evading punishment for his crimes? It seemed too many had simply gotten away with their despicable acts.

When Moeder returned to Amsterdam, she resumed her role as head of our family and started making plans for the future. The sense of normalcy changed. My mother was also quartered in the Joodse Invalide building in Amsterdam, sharing a room with other women. We three boys stayed in our accommodations. On the surface, daily life continued as it had been. However, I could no longer do whatever I wanted, was no longer a free bird. Now, I had to answer to my mother.

Years later, she confided in me that she never believed she would be able to look after us without my father, and that's why she complied with the suggestion of her family to move to Switzerland where she grew up and where her father and four brothers were living. So, about three or four months after our reunion, the four of us found ourselves living with my grandfather in a small apartment in Zurich, Switzerland.

From that point on, one might say, we settled into the new routine of daily life similar to the time preceding the war. There was a well-organized school, with books, notebooks, watercolor painting – all things I hadn't seen for years. It was so different from the provisional post-war school in Amsterdam. There were the afternoons and the hanging out with friends. We were sort of a survivor gang. There were regular evening meals around the table. Sometimes when I came home from school, there was a delicious smell of cake floating through the kitchen, cakes that Moeder was baking. There were the family gatherings on Sundays, and there was vacation…

You could call it a return to normalcy.

But the return to normal turned out not to be easy, not for us and not for anybody else.

We had to adapt to the change, to a totally new country. We faced people who looked at us differently (and treated us differently). After all, we were something "special" – we were Holocaust survivors. People talked and behaved toward us as if walking on eggshells and looked at us with some sort of guilt written all over their faces. Everybody, it seemed, was sorry, and strangely enough, we made them uncomfortable. There was this constant hush-hush around us that made us angry. At school, everything was different, the school system, the teaching system, the dress code, and worst of all the language; Zurich is located in the German-speaking part of Switzerland.

I remember that first day I entered the classroom. One of my classmates leaped to his feet and called out loud in German: "*Achtung!*" (Attention!), and everybody got to their feet as the teacher came in. We stood rigidly still till he gave us permission to sit back down. Hearing the boy's voice shouting in German *"Achtung!"* I froze. It took me back to the endless roll calls in Bergen-Belsen. I felt terrorized again. When I got home, I told Moeder to just forget it, I was not going back to that school. Period. It took her a good couple of days to finally convince me to go back.

There is an old Yiddish proverb: "Man plans, and God laughs."

Here I was, a Holocaust survivor trying hard to forget the past, promising myself from day one to boycott anything that was connected to the Germans or Germany, and I now found myself living in a country where Swiss-German – a kind of German dialect – was spoken and where official documents, newspapers, and schoolbooks were printed in the German language. Although after a while I got used to it, I still despise the language. I won't read books in German to this day.

For many years after the war, Germany and German goods were taboo to me. Under no circumstances would I travel to Germany, buy German products, or watch German TV. But as they say, life goes on and things change. And what about people? – I am not so sure about that.

I spent years in the United States, but returned to Switzerland in the 1960s when Moeder fell seriously ill, started my own business, married, and fathered three boys, all grown up now with children of their own. That's what you call *naches* – proud enjoyment. Today I live with my wife in Israel.

My business led me to spend a great deal of time with people of different nationalities. There were also German businesspeople whom I could not ignore. From the beginning, when meeting an elderly German man, pleasant and courteous, I'd immediately ask myself: *Where were you during the war? Are you a Nazi in disguise?* And later on, when meeting younger ones, I'd keep asking myself: *Was this man's father an SS man?*

It wasn't pleasant to think this way, but I think the underlying reason must have been that I simply loathed speaking the German language. Though admittedly, age and experience and life did soften me.

I learned to deal with it. They say things change and people change. I know that not everything in life is black and white, and I no longer look at every German as a potential Nazi. However, for me, everything that has to do with Germany and Germans still gives me the creeps. After all, Germany was the birthplace of Nazism – the source of the worst of all possible evils.

Once, while on a business trip to Frankfurt, Germany, I felt myself drawn to revisit Bergen-Belsen. I didn't plan to do it, but as I was already in Germany, after checking in to the hotel, the thought crossed my mind, *Why not go?* Why not revisit the place where I had been as a boy, imprisoned for almost two years. I had not been back since.

Now, it seemed something wanted me to bid farewell to my father, to my friends. Like a magnet, it kept pulling me back to the former concentration camp. The camp was located up north near the town of Bremen, several hundred kilometers from Frankfurt, more or less. *Might take a two- or three-hour train ride, not more... Yes, why not go?*

I recall when the cab driver pulled up to the Intercontinental Hotel and I stepped out and saw two elderly, well-dressed men engaged in conversation in front of the hotel, again, I wondered immediately: Where had they been during the war?

In the lobby, when checking in, hearing the German language again, it struck me forcibly. Like an echo of the past, it reverberated in my mind. The *Bitte schön*, and *Danke schön*, exactly the way they used to talk, grovelingly polite. Although I usually lived my life with the past safely compartmentalized, as if it had happened to someone else, now I couldn't separate it from me.

On the third day of my visit, I inquired at the front desk about trains going to Hamburg. The quickest train, they said, would be three and a half hours, and I could get a cheaper fare at the desk. I nodded. I would rent a car at the railroad station in Hamburg. The ride to the memorial, the desk clerk told me after consulting the roadmap, would take about one hour. "What about a hotel?" I asked him. "I might stay at a hotel overnight."

The young desk clerk smiled politely. "No problem, sir." He could book everything – train, hotel, and car. Like they say, the Germans are famous for their efficiency.

The next day, I was ready to go. It was a sunny summer day in late July 1970.

Seeing Germany after so many years was astonishing. Everything had changed. I recalled the ruins as Germany was flattened by the relentless Allied bombing and people wandered around homeless in the rubble. Now, now everything looked like a different country altogether. I recognized nothing. Modern new buildings lined the three- and four-lane streets. There were shiny-looking BMW and Mercedes cars. Ritzy-looking hotels and shops were filled with expensive goods. It was a different, opulent Germany; nothing was recognizable.

The train ride went along the scenic Rhine River and the famous and beautiful Lorelei Valley, surround by birch-covered hills. After a trip of three and half hours, I rented a car at a Hertz car rental at the Hamburg railway station, asked for a roadmap, and then set off for the memorial.

The camp surroundings – the tall pine woods beyond the flat grain fields – seemed intensely familiar as I pulled up to the memorial gate. Just the way I remembered it, *exactly the way it was*, I thought, feeling a knot in my stomach. I got out and walked toward the entrance where under a small stand of trees a large brick wall stood with the inscription "Gedenkstätte Bergen-Belsen" (Bergen-Belsen Memorial). I looked at a sign on the wall that read: "To the hell of Bergen-Belsen." Under it, some angry graffitist had written, "Welcome to the human race!"

A middle-aged man in overalls came through the gate and got on a bike. He was one of the people who tended the camp grounds. He was about to start down the road, but stopped, turned his head, and asked me where I came from. I told him. "Have you ever been in Germany before?" he wanted to know, in accented English. His eyes were staring at me curiously. I nodded yes. I once lived here, I said. Long time ago. In the war. Nodding, his eyes turned flat. "The world has changed since then," he told me, "and much has changed here. You will find us different. We are different people today." *Yeah, right*, I thought, and watched him ride off on his bicycle.

I turned, took a deep breath, and went through the gate and stared. I no longer knew where I was. Where were the rows of barracks, the barbed-wire fence, the SS, the hated watch towers? As I stared at the large expanse of green, lush fields and the stone walkways and the surrounding woods, I tried to picture how it had been then, twenty-seven years earlier, when I had been imprisoned here with my father, mother, and two brothers. Typhus and other diseases had spread through the camp, which caused the British troops shortly after liberating the camp to burn down the barracks and everything around them.

Off to my left was the brown museum building, and I decided to go there first. Inside, visitors stood in silence talking in hushed voices as they gazed wide-eyed at brightly lit pictures displayed behind glass walls. I stood and stared at the photos, pictures that were all too familiar to me. Many photos were taken by British military amateur photographers at the time of the liberation. There were pictures of the victims' clothes, of jewelry, watches, and diaries that had been hidden by victims. I looked at the photos, carefully studying each one of them and staring at the people whose faces were memorialized there. I knew them, I had lived like them. My heart went out to them – to the ones who had succumbed to the agonizing suffering and to the ones who survived – and for a moment, tears welled up and I had to fight them back.

There was an often shown photo of German civilians from a nearby town – boys and girls, disbelieving old men, and young women – forced by furious battle-hardened American soldiers to file past a line of skeletal corpses of Jewish prisoners who had been starved to death in a concentration camp. Some of the civilians had their eyes lowered in shame, while others simply turned their faces away.

I turned to the next picture, a group of the fifty SS guards, among them coarse-faced, bull-necked Commandant Josef Kramer, the last commandant at the Birkenau death camp, and the notoriously cruel Irma Grese, a twenty-one-year-old guard who had been a member of the staff at the Auschwitz camp. I looked for the young guard Pavlenko and for Aufseherin Krumm, but I did not see them in the photos. Where had they gone? Had they slipped away and escaped the Allies before the camp was liberated?

Looking at the faces of Kramer and of Grese, these two barbarians (I remember seeing both in the camp), just watching them was shocking, deeply frightening. I asked myself: *Have today's Germans changed in any way? I mean, there are both bad and good eggs in a basket, so maybe you'd better not generalize. That's right.* I nodded. *Better be careful with judgment. But my God, if I recall what they did to my family, how can I judge objectively? I simply can't.* And that's the truth, that's the reality.

And don't forget, there's one other thing. I'll tell you what I mean. When, like now, you stare at these two beastly humans – they are not really humans, they are true animals – this Kramer and Grese, just think of what that SS Aufseherin Krumm did to us. How she extended her arm, pointing a finger at my family and imperiously ordering us to stay – STAY! – and we couldn't leave the camp on that train to freedom, had to stay behind in the camp. How can I judge Germans any differently? *But hey*, I reminded myself, *that's the way it is. Once you experienced all that horror and saw what these people could do to you, murder you in cold blood. Just remember.*

Of course, I thought, listening to my inner voice, *I remember. I do. I recall all of it.* I can see it before my eyes: the floggings with leather whips, the beatings with rubber pipes. And not to forget other atrocities I learned about later, the cruelest torture the SS had on hand, the lethal injections and drowning in pools. *Keep all that clearly in mind, so you won't forget, okay?* That these inhuman punishments were often meted out in front of the prisoners standing there in freezing weather lined up for roll call. And after I listed all these heroic deeds, how can anyone with common sense even think of these people as being law-abiding citizens? How preposterous. And to add fuel to the fire, so to speak, how long could it have lasted before someone somewhere rose up and proclaimed the Holocaust never happened? Everything, they say, is an invented lie. I know people. I know what they are capable of, so I can't be surprised.

I turned and walked out of the building, and once I was outside, moving around the former camp grounds, the floodgates opened up. For fifteen months, this place, this Nazi death camp, had been my home. I looked around the long stretches of green fields, the trees and pinewoods. And that's about it. Everything else was gone. The Brits had made a good job of burning everything down when they arrived.

I started walking down along the brick walkways and gazed at the small burial mounds with the little metal plaques that were scattered across the grassy grounds; five thousand buried here…ten thousand there…fifteen thousand over there…then twenty thousand…it didn't stop.

Visitors were wandering through the well-tended grounds. Some stood in solemn silence in front of a tall obelisk. I stood there a long moment on the grass and looked at the scene in front of me. It's hard to give a full picture of what that place meant to me. The trees. Those beautiful beech trees and those oak trees. I had faced them for fifteen months. Now I said hello them. They seemed to talk to me. *Remember*, they told me, *we were here*. The trees had witnessed what happened here.

I pulled myself away and started walking around the vast grounds. After I had studied the display case of the former camp inside the building, I knew roughly where I was. I stood in the spot where the roll call square had once been. I had stood here in the rain and freezing weather listening to the obscene expletives and hollering voices of the SS men. I stood here looking out at that SS guard savagely beating Moeder with a billy club. I was here and ran across the quadrangle as the Allied planes had attacked the camp.

Now, the area looked almost like a peaceful picnic spot. No human skeletons were visible, no barbed-wire fence. Where once stood the barracks and the watch towers were now grain fields and forests. And silence. And for a moment in my mind's eye, I spotted the bony prisoners standing on the roll call square in rows of five or lying on the bunkbeds sick, dying, like ghosts, here where I once sat with my dying buddies, talking and dreaming about food.

All these people, I thought, my friends, Uriel and Kees, they were not numbers. They just wanted to live like everybody else and got mercilessly murdered, their young lives wasted. They seemed to cry out, to tell the world not to forget…

My father was lying here somewhere in one of the mass graves – or was he cremated in the furnace? I pictured Vader dying in the hospital ward and being carted off on a stretcher in the middle of the night by two men of the burial unit. Standing there, the stillness engulfing me, I felt the tears well up in my eyes and I cried. Cried for what they had done to him, cried for not having been able to cry at the time. Trying hard to control my emotions, I clenched my teeth, wiped the tears away, and slowly, softly, I began to recite Kaddish, a prayer for my father and for all those who were lying here who had died at the hands of their Nazi tormentors.

Before I left, I visited the documentation center, the main exhibition hall, the House of Silence, and the film tower, which showed films about Bergen-Belsen and its liberation. Large groups of young people visited the camp. Busloads of German students talking in hushed voices arrived with their teachers. I read from a colored pamphlet that there were guided tours available in German, English, French, Dutch, Spanish, and Hungarian.

Watching the German youngsters, I had mixed emotions. *Will they continue the fight against this evil by every means possible? Or will they glorify this wickedness and just shut their eyes and ears as did most Germans?*

On the way out, casting a last glance at the place for several seconds, I thought of the song "Last Goodbye." I walked out the exit and stopped at the cafeteria on the ground floor for a cup of coffee.

It was getting dark when I pulled the little blue car out onto the road and headed to Celle, where I was booked in the Ringhotel Celler Tor for the night. The ride lasted twenty minutes. When I drove past the old, now vacant loading platform, for a moment the past rose up again; it was here that Moeder, my two brothers, and I got evacuated from the camp in trucks and boarded the train that was to become known as the Lost Train.

I leaned over and switched on the car radio just in time to hear a news broadcast that in the Middle East, the Israeli Air Force had shot down five Soviet MIG fighter jets over Syria.

My chest swelled in pride thinking of Israel, and my heart went out to the country and its people warmly. I listened for five more minutes before turning off the radio.

When I checked into the Ringhotel Celler Tor, there was a long line at the front desk in the lobby. There was a big convention staying in the hotel, the girl told me as she handed me the keys for the room. I was glad I had booked ahead.

My room, on the second floor, was big and comfortable. That night I felt strange, lying in a German bed in a German hotel, fourteen miles (23 km) away from the place where I had suffered so much as a boy. My eyes kept staring at the dark ceiling. But it was the right thing to do, coming back and revisiting the camp. In a way, I felt I was bearing witness. I had come back to Bergen-Belsen to tell the world what had happened, so we won't forget.

The next morning, the main dining room was filled with convention attendees. Five guests sat down together at the table next to mine. Many people at the tables seemed to know one another. Some of them were standing around, sharing thoughts. There was a self-service buffet and salad bar. Waiters were busy getting drinks from the bar for some guests. There was a soft hum of talk and the clinking of dishes. I had a grilled vegetarian sandwich and a cup of coffee.

I didn't feel at ease, not at all. I was sitting with German people who were slurping beers and eating ham and eggs with cheese and sausages, digging ravenously into the pile of food that was on the plates before them while not far from here, a mere twelve miles away, my father was lying in a mass grave or had been cremated after having been starved to death by these gentlemen. Hey, maybe one of them, a former SS man, was right here, sitting at the table, enjoying the fresh-baked bread and made-to-order eggs and omelets? I glanced around and saw a few elderly men and wondered which of them might have been at the Belsen or Auschwitz camps. The mere thought made me lose my appetite, and quietly I placed my fork and knife beside my plate.

At the table next to me was loud laughter. I turned to look and saw two women and three men in conversation, one of the men pointing to a newspaper one of them had been reading, which now lay folded over on the table. Sufficiently understanding German, I realized that they were talking about the tension between Israel and Syria after Israeli planes had shot down Soviet fighter jets in Syria. The man who had put the paper aside said one word, *die Drecksjuden*, the *filthy Jews*, and one of the women burst into gleeful laughter.

Feeling the blood rush to my head, I got to my feet. They were now saying something about Hitler and the gas ovens. I looked across at them, threw down my napkin in disgust, and for a moment, just for a moment, wanted to walk up to them and start an argument – maybe even pick a fight, I didn't give a damn. But I stopped and shrugged. *You want to pick a fight with these Germans, good luck, be my guest.* It probably would have ended in an ugly brawl that I'd have lost badly anyway. Feeling a wave of rage and disgust come over me, I walked out of the dining room. Twenty-five years after the savage murder of millions of people and the liberation of the camps, the tune had not changed at all.

It took me only a few minutes to pack. I went down to the lobby and checked out. As I was driving back to Hamburg in my small blue coupe, I thought about the Germans at the table next to me. *The world has learned nothing. Nada. Zero.*

My wife told me later that when I arrived home, I was in a state of shock, acted as if I were in a trance, didn't communicate, and just kept to myself. She was right. It took me a good couple of days till I managed to wriggle out of it and got back into my daily routine.

I still wonder how an entire nation with a rich history and fine culture such as Germany could have plummeted into the abyss of cruel murder and organized barbarism. I am fully aware that not all Germans were killers. With the passage of time, I have learned to get along well with new generations of German people. But...deep down inside, right or wrong, I don't trust them. And I certainly cannot forgive or forget the death of my father and the misery and suffering and pain we endured.

Against all odds, I survived the Holocaust and, in time, recovered and could provide a good life for me and my family. Nevertheless, I'll be aware of the evil that lurks.

The following thought gives me great comfort: I am the living proof that evil does not triumph. My children and future generations descended from survivors will make sure the world will never forget the horrors wrought by Nazi fanaticism.

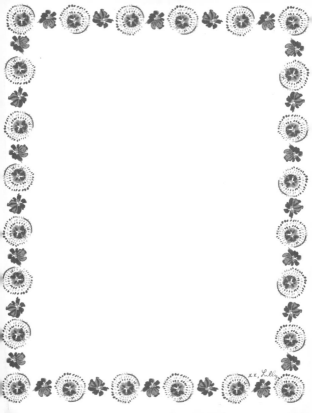

x x, Lilly